The Four Seasons

Edited by: A.J. Huffman
and April Salzano

Cover Art: "The Four Seasons" collage by Nate Dworsky & A.J. Huffman

Copyright © 2015 A.J. Huffman

All rights reserved. Except for brief quotations in critical articles or reviews, no part of this book may be reproduced in any manner without prior written permission from the publisher:

Kind of a Hurricane Press
www.kindofahurricanepress.com
kindofahurricanepress@yahoo.com

CONTENTS

Featured Piece

Tracy Davidson	*A Leaf for All Seasons*	19

From the Authors

Jonel Abellanosa	*Thirteen Ways of Looking*	23
Trevor Alexander	*Spring Haibun*	25
Kara Arguello	*Pennsylvania, October*	26
	That September	27
Carol Alena Aronoff	*Autumn in Honaunau*	28
	A Devotional	29
	Winter Offering	30
Allen Ashley	*Summer on Pluto*	31
Michael Ashley	*Bell Tower*	32
Steve Ausherman	*Flashes of Dry Lightning*	33
Donna Barkman	*Autumn Walk*	35
	Plagarists	36
Emily Bartholet	*Portrait of My Sister*	37
Jonathan Beale	*Spring Days Passing*	38
Colin Bell	*Gardening Tips*	39
Nina Bennett	*A Daughter's Plea*	40
Stefanie Bennett	*Eucalypt Dreaming*	41

Karen Berry	Epithalmion Seasons	42
Suzette Bishop	New York City Ballet Summers in Saratoga	43
	Tacking in 110°	44
	Kayaking on Big Sur	46
Jane Blanchard	Untitled	47
Larry Blazek	Two Hawks	48
Irene Bloom	Migration	49
	Lost and Found	50
Barbara Brooks	Window	52
	Summer Train	53
Michael H. Brownstein	The Seasons of Death	54
	Winter's Harvest	55
	One Day the Witch of the Winter Gave Gifts to Her Neighbors	56
Tanya Bryan	Winter, Sort Of	57
Wayne F. Burke	Zero	58
Miki Byrne	Winter is a Dark Room	59
Janet Rice Carnahan	The Dance	60
Alan Catlin	Post Card Poem to S from Block Island	61
	Listening to Vivaldi's Four Seasons at Outdoor Amphitheater as the Sun Goes Down	62

Aidan Clarke	*Seasons in the Cemetery*	63
	Flying South	65
	The Cuckoo Leaves Home	67
	Long Ago Autumn	69
Sharon Cote	*For My Friends, While It's Still Chilly*	70
	The Old Well in the Front Yard	71
Chella Courington	*Snow Angel*	72
Linda M. Crate	*The Seasons Took All They Had Come For*	73
	Frosty Proposal	75
Wayne Cresser	*Burning Frost, Happy Day!*	76
Betsey Cullen	*Soup*	78
Graham Curtis	*The Fall*	79
Oliver Cutshaw	*Dogwoods in Boston*	80
Susan Dale	*October*	81
	September, Glorious Stranger	82
	Autumn 2014	83
Lela Marie De La Garza	*Summer*	84
Brindley Hallam Dennis	*The Penitent*	85
Julie A. Dickson	*Seasons Passed*	87
Joseph Dorazio	*The End of Summer*	88

William Doreski	*October's Retro Gaze*	89
	Gloomy Winter Pools	91
	The Dead of Winter	93
J.K. Durick	*Heat*	95
Leixyl Kaye Emmerson	*71 Sermons*	96
Zach Fechter	*Wheat*	97
Sharon Fedor	*Anticipation at Lake Overlook*	98
Michael Freveletti	*Snow Maiden*	99
Jason Gallagher	*Seasonal Affective Sestina*	102
Susan Gardner	*First Flush*	104
Brigitte Goetze	*Digging Potatoes in August*	105
Elissa Gordon	*Bad Weather*	106
	How to Plant a Tribute Garden	107
	A Perfectly Good Day	108
Ray Greenblatt	*Coastal Winter*	109
	7°	110
John Grey	*A Warm Day in February*	111
	Last Snowflake in Spring	113
Pat Hanahoe-Dosch	*Fall*	114
	Detritus	115
William Ogden Haynes	*Between Seasons*	116

Eileen Holmes	*What's Beautiful Anyway?*	118
Ruth Holzer	*January*	120
Carol Hornak	*Unfrozen*	121
Susan Martell Huebner	*The Summer of the Epidemic*	122
	Red Barn	123
Liz Hufford	*The Promise of Heat*	124
S.E. Ingraham	*Swan Song for Winter*	125
M.J. Iuppa	*Lift Bridge*	126
	The Way Home	127
Evie Ivy	*The Seasons in Four Cinquains*	128
Diane Jackman	*Still The Year Turns . . .*	129
Juli Jana	*Winter Sequence*	130
	Summer Street	132
	I Had Always Wondered About Knots in Trees in Spring	133
Michael Lee Johnson	*April Winds*	134
	Even as Evening	135
	Fall is Golden	136
Claire Keyes	*My Caribbean*	137
	Come September	139
	Molly	140

Lori Kiefer	*Summer and You*	142
	Autumn Returns	143
	Untitled	144
Phyllis Klein	*The Spring Curmudgeon Realizes What Comes Next*	145
Steve Klepetar	*The Summer I Was Ten*	146
Julie Kovacs	*Summer in the Everglades*	147
Tricia Knoll	*Through Flames in the New Year's Fire*	148
Kevin Kreiger	*The Counting of Blessing*	151
Veronica Lake	*Winter Afternoon, Café Strip, Fremantle*	155
Martha Landman	*Come to Me*	156
	I Never Wanted to Leave	157
	Of Rain and Skin and Cloud	158
Mark Lewis	*The Quickening of Seasons*	159
Lyn Lifshin	*Heron on Ice*	162
	Geese on Ice	163
	Before Any Snow	164
	Trying to Just Smell the Tangerine Tree's Blossoms	165
	Walking Past the Pond at Night	166
Lennart Lundh	*Chronophobic Triptych*	167

Hillary Lyon	*Sometimes Love is Copious*	169
	Milagrosa	170
	Magnetic Bee	171
Don Mager	*August Journal: Tuesday, August 6, 2013*	172
Stacy Lynn Mar	*Snapshot Summer*	173
	Blue Moons in Spring	175
	Dreams of the Fisherman's House	176
	Autumn Night	178
Adam Marks	*Climate Change You Can Believe In*	179
Jackie Davis Martin	*Seasons*	180
Amanda M. May	*Stone with Memory*	182
Bob McNeil	*Anopheles*	185
Joan McNerney	*Beach*	186
Karla Linn Merrifield	*Sold*	187
Dilip Mohapatra	*Summer Love*	189
Ralph Monday	*Of Firewood and Winter Sky*	190
	September	191
	The Winter Solstice	192
	The Hearer	193
	Moontime in Blood	194

Wilda Morris	*Late February Snow*	195
	In the January Chill	196
Carol Murphy	*Claire and the Wind*	197
Joseph Murphy	*Black Ice*	199
Lee Nash	*Four Seasons Haiku*	200
Jude Neale	*Tongue Speak*	201
Mary Newell	*Spring Dead*	203
Reeve Nicholls	*Morning of All Mornings*	204
BZ Niditch	*Wild Roses*	207
	Constable's Landscapes	208
Suzanne O'Connell	*Freesia in Winter*	209
Norman J. Olson	*The Crab Apple Tree*	211
	Spring: Is Anybody Listening to the Trees?	212
Carl Palmer	*Shadow Lake Snow Snakes*	213
Joyce Parkes	*Engaging Vancouver, BC*	214
Simon Perchik	*Untitled*	215
Richard King Perkins II	*The Plains of Venezuela*	216
	Autumn in Aqua Immemorial	217

Georgia Ressmeyer	*Winter into Spring*	219
	Summer Doldrums	220
	Eyes on Fire	221
Pippa Rowen	*England Through the Seasons*	222
Tom Russell	*Untitled*	225
	Wallpaper	226
Mary Salen	*Ode to the August Rose Bush*	227
Paul Sasges	*Teeming*	228
Francesca Sasnaitis	*My Dead*	229
Emily Jo Scalzo	*Untitled*	230
	Untitled	231
Zvi A. Sesling	*Blizzard*	232
Jo Simons	*Winter*	233
Rosemary Marshall Staples	*Even Sins*	234
Tom Sterner	*Grand Seasons & Grandsons*	235
	Promenade	236
Jeanine Stevens	*The Garden of Tuileries on a Winter Afternoon*	237
	The Water Table – November	238

Emily Strauss	*Winter Arrives*	240
	Spring Coming	241
	The First Rains	242
Smita Sriwastav	*Seasons*	243
	I Am a Changing Dream	246
Neelamani Sutar	*Spring*	250
	An Indian Summer	252
Fanni Sütő	*Winter Solstice*	254
Anne Swannell	*The Poet Observes Quota Compliance, Take-Overs and Net Capital Loss in Her Spring Garden*	255
	Needles	256
	Cyanocitta Cristata	257
	The Ice Breakers	258
	Listening to Ravel's Bolero While Two Leaves Spin Outside My Window	260
Marianne Szlyk	*The Holly Tree in Summer*	261
	At the Almost Empty Vegetarian Café	262
Susan Tally	*Sag Harbor, After a Long Habit of Turning Down Invitations to Visit People in Their Summer Places*	263
Sarah Thursday	*What I Mean When I Say Ageless*	264

Dennis Trujillo	When Winter Lingers Past the Solstice	265
Tesia Tsai	Civil War	266
Marion Turner	Magnolias	267
Lorette Diane Walker	Watching from the Chair by the Window	268
Toren Wallace	Telling Each Other They are Loved	269
Mercedes Webb-Pullman	The Four Seasons	270
	Seasons of Love	271
	Making a Poem #7	272
Mary L. Westcott	Winter Walk	273
Joanna M. Weston	Secret Stache	274
	Gardener's Return	275
	One Clean Sheet	276
Dan Wilcox	Winter Argument	277
Martin Willitts, Jr.	Grandmother Spider Sews the Fabric of the Seasons Together	278
Laura Madeline Wiseman	Bird Charm	281
Phil Wood	Pippin	282
Mantz Yorke	Appalachian Spring	283
	The Blossoming, Kopelovo, 1986	284
	Snowscape, River Usk	285

Changming Yuan	*Seasonal Stanzas*	286
	Summerscape	288
	Autumnscape	289
	Winterscape	290

From the Editors

A.J. Huffman	*Walking with Wings*	293
	An Unscheduled Change in Persona	294
	Lake Huron Rocks	295
	The Path	296
	Spring Released	297
	I Am Leaf	298
	Daily Downpour	299
	The Signs of Spring	300
	The Cold Hand of Winter	301
April Salzano	*December, 2013*	302
	Goodbye September	303
	It's Just What We Do (Winters Up North)	304
	For One Son	305
	Smelling God	306
	Smelling Stinkbug	307

I Am Going to Kick April's Ass	308
July and My Mother's Twin	309
The Day was Buried	310
Author Bios	313
About the Editors	345

Featured Piece

This anthology's featured piece represents the editors' choice for the best artistic interpretation of the theme of seasons (Spring, Summer, Autumn, Winter), and for that reason, the editors feel it deserves special focus.

A Leaf for all Seasons (a haiku sequence)

Spring

verdant leaves
and apple blossom
the bleat of lambs

young lovers
row riverboats
beside weeping willows

Summer

leaves of lace
all that's left behind
by caterpillars

a lone fisherman
waits on the riverbank
for rainbows

Autumn

leaves crunch underfoot
disturbing nuts half-buried
in the cooling ground

river traffic
the strident honking
of departing geese

Winter

branches bare of leaves
skeletal fingers
reaching for the sky

young lovers
carve hearts
in rivers of ice

-- Tracy Davidson

From The Authors

Thirteen Ways of Looking

1. rain singing all week
heart's hermit thrush
voiceless

2. taste of tea
white as perched
serendipity

3. fiction writing—
indoor branches
for angelic beings

4. insight:
elusive
flowerpecker

5. raindrops
too many commas
for a fruitless day

6. smell of coffee . . .
memory
drinking from its feathers

7. chirps in the downpour—
mind full
of parables

8. curtain turning like a page . . .
where's the pterodactyl
in the mirror?

9. window
with tricks of trees—
foretelling sparrows

10. hot cocoa . . .
metaphors following flocks
searching their songleader

11. I don't know which to prefer, woods for my winged beings or a
poem with moon in the pond. I rummage my drawers for the winter we
don't have, well-versed in the monsoon's dialogues with our summer
sun glowing like Mandarin orange. To imagine the dry spell, I try iced
and milked blends: cantaloupe-papaya, apple-soursop, dragon fruit-
mango.

Odus the Owl . . .
darkened room
for nestled warmth

12. Butterflies on my vision's
hibiscus: echoes
of the storm's beauty

13. Maybe the songbird
was the orange light
on the field of grass

-- Jonel Abellanosa

*Author's Note: Odus the Owl is part of the popular game Candy Crush
Saga*

Spring Haibun

Land relaxes in denial of winter's clenched claw. Fragile seeming shoots bravely thrust through thawing earth. Vanguard crocuses dot meadows with bright color, contrasting slender snowdrops. Migrating birds return and pair off, renovating vacant nests. Reprobate magpies huddle in groups discussing latest thefts. Early lambs caper around their mothers in lolloping leaps, oblivious to the world. Melting snows coupled with errant showers swell streams and rivers, burbling between brimming banks. Mountains slowly bare their heads of icy bonnets under welcome warming sun. Nature's urgency drives single-minded passion of new life for old, frozen death of old year giving way to burgeoning life of new.

Floral tapestry
Painting fast waking meadow
Nature's renaissance

-- Trevor Alexander

Pennsylvania, October

" . . . fitfully wander, when the wild leaves loosen . . ."

-- Rainer Maria Rilke

When the air smells of chimney smoke,
and the children run through the yard
in bright jackets, wild as turkeys,
it's easy to notice:
Summer fades so quickly,
leaves red-gold forests in return.
Loosen your fists;
breathe.

-- Kara Arguello

That September

After you left
I set my face to the river
and stayed that way for hours.

My head lay on the muddy bank,
my body half out of green-dark water,
a reluctant mermaid.

The river, huge and violent,
dragged with it everything
which could be torn loose from the earth.

Ripped from their moorings,
whole docks washed downstream. Boats
dangled like fish on a line.

How could I,
not a strong swimmer,
possibly have held fast?

-- Kara Arguello

Autumn in Honaunau

First cool day in October
and the rain is insistent,
washing dust from summer
leaves while puddling
on the tin roof,
indifferent to the plight
of leaking crevices.

A pause in the downpour;
the air is tight as if holding
its breath awaiting
the next deluge, knowing
it will free debris from roof
gutters and bring the nearby
river to its knees.

-- Carol Alena Aronoff

A Devotional

Spring is a witch in trollop's clothing
wearing white gloves to church. Demure
as a schoolgirl, wild as unfettered joy.
Uncontainable yet married to the limits
of constellations watching from afar.

No one wears a sunflower in their hair.
Only sages sit by streams and whistle
feathers. Spring has captured my spirit
in her web of freedom and flung me
to the outer reaches of Sylvanus' lair.

Contradictions run riot and where
they come together and mix, small
miracles bloom. Snowmelt, cold bluster,
soft rain and strengthening sun conspire
in the sweet fragrance of hyacinth.

Mood swings and reveries, a sudden
longing for strawberries and I am
running for my seedlings and shovel.
So much is germinating, waiting to
burst forth beyond my usual reticence.

Fairy grass is sprouting from my hair.
Gardenias drape the hem of my cotton voile
dress. I dance with tree sisters, chant with
cardinals in the wind. Moving with the force
of the season, I am once again untamed.

-- *Carol Alena Aronoff*

Winter Offering

Under a harsh light moon, trees huddle
together on the cusp of hill, draped in sage
and olive wool to mute the whispering chill.
Even rocks are dressed for winter,
flaunting moss blankets.
I wander among silvered leaves, amid silence
so stark, my thoughts are shrill notes
of comic opera. If I could banish them
to a cave where brown bears hibernate,
what would I be left with?
My mind stills as snow not yet fallen;
for a moment there is only space,
radiant joy which warms the cloud-banked
dark with faintest light, a subtle reminder
of sacred ground.
I open myself–arms, great wings–
to soften brittle wind that threatens
to upend nests of thrush, send
shivering rose petals to an early death.
Who will read my body as living prayer?

-- *Carol Alena Aronoff*

Summer on Pluto

Despite our eccentric orbit,
Summer on Pluto
is not recognizably any different
to Winter on Pluto.
We have to remind ourselves that
the distant twinkler is meant to be
our warming sun;
but barely offers light,
never mind heat.
Don't come here if you don't
like it Kelvin cold,
dark and airless.

To be fair,
our main concern is not the weather
or the climate;
it's those know-it-alls on Earth
who first of all classed us as
            a planet
then downgraded us
and lumped us together
with Ceres and other post-Neptunian rocks as,
wait for it,
"plutoids".
We get all their broadcasts and mutterings.
One day these Earth sorts
will come visit us
and we'll have strong words to say.
It might be Summer for us
but it will be Winter for them.

-- Allen Ashley

Bell Tower

penis-like
swording upward to the sky

I light a smoke
watch lambs sitting flush
against a dry stone wall

the lush groin of countryside

the protracted shadow
a dark phallus laid across the rise

I blow smoke rings
they're reflections

the slow separation
of seasons
of delicate trappings

a rim of soft lips
draw breath
draw breath
then die

-- Michael Ashley

Flashes of Dry Lightning

Winter

Even though she never wanted heroic end-of-life measures, the machine was now breathing for her. What was once the natural and silent workings of lung and esophagus, bronchi and trachea, nose and throat, larynx and tongue were now the oiled machinery of electricity-powered digital beeps, tubes and wires, and an unnatural, rhythmic expansion and contraction of her chest cavity. She was 71.

Spring

Despite the diligent sponge-baths of the nurses and the daily room cleaning of the custodial staff, the hospital room had begun to take on a smell that was a combination of body odor, disinfectant, clean sheets, decay, and plastic. The letters, balloons and flowers that had filled the room in January, from former co-workers and friends, were now replaced with the sterile glow of light coming through a window, and a vase with a single flower that was weekly replaced by her best friend, her only friend, her lifetime friend, the only one who has remained.

Summer

It rained the day of the funeral. She was buried behind a church next to the graves of her parents. At the age of nine, she received her first kiss amidst these cold tombstones by a young boy, freckly and sweet, during a short recess between evening Vacation Bible School classes. His lips were dry and they pecked out at her like a frog snapping its tongue at a fly. The air held the humidity and bugs of a July evening, and there were flashes of dry lightning on the western horizon. It was a sweet and strange way to experience a first kiss. Life and death, innocence and longing, Bible passages and the devil hiding in desire, freckles and giggles, fireflies arising and a distant storm. Seven people showed up at the funeral, if you count the minister and the man who operated the backhoe. As the cars pulled out of the parking lot, mounds of earth were already falling down hard, from the backhoe bucket, on the pine box of her casket.

Fall

The mouse couldn't easily see the sky as it moved between the tombstones. Feeding on the high grasses that rose against the stones, where the blades of the mower couldn't reach, the mouse didn't see the shadow of the Red-Tailed hawk falling from the sky on its way to envelop her. The tombstones were cold. To the bird they were white boulders. The inscriptions of names and dates upon the marble faces were simple patterns to avian eyes. His beak was covered in blood. The tombstone shadows angled outwards in geometric perfection.

-- Steve Ausherman

Autumn Walk

Her beagle nose reads the dry leaves
like the morning paper, assiduous
tracking of last night's passages,
    tales of mayhem and chase.
We slow the pace, our noses high,
mine to inhale the lusty scent of decay,
    the brittle chill of October air,
hers to perform the complicated
    analytics of a chemical engineer.
We crunch along on the color wheel
of Fall leaves, every shade but blue,
    saved for the sky.

-- Donna Barkman

Plagiarists

The branches of the pussy willow tree
      grown huge from clippings
      planted decades ago
thrash in the unrelenting blasts
         of a punctual March wind

Tiny tight buds labor forth their furry tips:
      daredevils—
destined to outwit snowdrops and crocus
daring to compete with today's storm
       their fuzzy torsos bigger than snow flakes
       and just as white

The intrepid catkins will puff up and fluff
      even as they divine the end
         of their circumscribed lives
when they'll too soon tumble to earth
       overworked, overblown and spent
while daffodils and violets and smartass
       forsythia smugly slip into the Spring
that the willows so pluckily announced

             -- Donna Barkman

Portrait of My Sister

A flutist with long hands
plucks quarter notes from the air
like Fuji apples.
She sets her harvest on a piano bench.
Allows her limbs to bow forward as if
curling into vines.

The musician orders her audience to sing.
Inhales the perfume
of little black fruits.

-- Emily Bartholet

Spring Days Passing...

In the seas pink shadow hangs over;
The blossom is as the lemmings live.
Falling in fallacy.
Staying nowhere, for too long.
In a childhood's disproportionate *modus operandi.*

The blossom: turning the tarmac pink.
The rain, adding its own hue.
The hearing and the knowing never the same thing.
The day is at the beginning, the adolescence of the year.
In a tantrum: of reasonableness – a storm.

The fertile hour, beholden, to histories paternity.
Always ignore tradition.
Upon a plate of nutritious platitudes;
Forgotten against the impending summer;
As we all swim in a pink blossom sea, in spring's days
passing....

-- Jonathan Beale

Gardening Tip

Seasons break their word so don't trust Nature's promises.
Fresh-sprung leaves mock grief with hope.
Forsythia blossom is an acid sneer.
Daffodil bulbs planted in Autumn won't ease our malaise.
When gaudy zinnias shrivel, death-blackened by frost,
we still have gold rush dreams, fingers warm in frozen earth.

-- Colin Bell

A Daughter's Plea

Four seasons. Let my mother
have four more seasons. Another
parade of magenta, lemon,
cinnamon lining her street. A puff
of cashmere caressing her neck,
warding off the crisp edge
of an October breeze.

May she wake to stillness,
street sounds muffled
by an overnight snow. We'll
light every lamp in the house,
chase the gloaming with Irish coffee.

Once more let her view her flower beds,
purple crocus nudging the earth aside.
Charms of pink and white bleeding hearts
dangle, dance, suspended above
unfurling fronds of ferns. Through
the open kitchen window,
may she inhale the spicy scent of peonies.

I want to sit with her on the patio,
swallow tart limeade as a hummingbird
hovers at the feeder, wings
shimmering in the midday heat of August,
breath as shallow and trembling as hers.

-- Nina Bennett

Eucalypt Dreaming

. . . In my cupped hands
A vestige of gum leaves—

Home to the troubadour
Cicada who droned

Through page-dark
December's atlas where

Summer was no more—
Shorn by

The cold kiln of primal
Decline, and

Once upon a time's
Cicumspect, yet

Human, opulence.

-- Stefanie Bennett

Epithalmion Seasons

The epithalmion for spring
when love and the world
are peeled like young trees
grow careless and brave
roots feeding shoots
entwined with abandon.

The epithalmion for fall
when love lays by
gathered in, enduring
grain golden and stored
lit by red leaves
and the promise of bounty.

The epithalmion for winter
a bold and frozen snow
and love, not glacial
but a swift, glinting silver
a freshet running under tundra
an unexpected celebration.

The epithalmion for summer
when love, like the world
is full-blown and heavy
drunk on the sun
dazzled b the long days
of heat and honey and wine.

The strong summer vine
holds the sweet green of spring
the red leaf of fall
the white peace of winter
holds them as you hold each other
my beautiful sister, my beautiful brother.

-- *Karen Berry*

New York City Ballet Summers in Saratoga

The staged forest
                    The real woods
Snow: cotton balls
                                                    falling,
            Blown by fans
Summer heat shriveled by a cooling night

Fragrant costumes
Keeping mud off my patent leathers
A bluing of stage lights
A blackening around the   open-air theater
A filmy draped canopy bed   glides
            Across the stage
                                        My own bed
My parasol of summer leaves

                                        Beauty sleeping

                    -- Suzette Bishop

Tacking in 110°

Hands shaking,
Sight blurry and off center,
Forehead slimy,
Leather smell,
Sweltering dogs arranged
Around saddles and saddle pads.

Searching,   searching,   searching,
Saddle with pink seat not there,
Lift smallest saddle with shortest stirrups
Off its stand, grunting.

Unhook,
Untangle,
Unknot bridle parts
And put together.

Saddle too loose and
Falls off his back,
Ease it onto his back, again,
Pull cinch, feet planted,
Pull again,
Fingers hurt,
Nails crack, break,
Top of head on fire,
Hair falling into my face,
Neck-sweat dripping.

Little boys run around,
My money helps feed them
for another month,
One hitting the other over
the head with a plastic water bottle.

Unbuckling stirrup,
Slide won't budge,
Horse neighing, *Get on with it*,
Teenage girls on horses wear fake smiles,
Think my horse is *super cute,*
Want to know if I'm riding,
How old is he,
Is he mine?
No.
One girl has my saddle.
Pink seat swirls around,
Rides off,
Gritty dust in my mouth.

Stirrups too long,
Saddle too loose,
No, I'm not riding today.

-- Suzette Bishop

Kayaking on Big Sur

"Ahhhhhhhhhh," Audrey heard the couple behind them exclaim as a large eye surfaced above the water to her right.

Paddling against the current, steering around kelp beds, feeling even fatter in the tight life-jacket hadn't really been her idea of how to spend her summer vacation. "Why don't you go kayaking?" her mother-in-law said brightly, although no one had been fishing for suggestions. Audrey's paddle angled more sharply at the water.

"Watch out! Here comes another kelp bed," Mark shouted from the seat behind her. He was paddling more vigorously so the lightweight kayak would avoid getting tangled in the kelp. It was *so* hard to see out here with lightning strikes of glimmers everywhere you looked.

The giant eye disappeared while blow-hole spray burst up from below, "Whewwwwwwwwww." More and more puffs of spray gathered around the couples in kayaks.

"Wow! Look at that," someone shouted.

Audrey realized something solid rather than watery was raising them up.

"Watch out, Aud!"

Fuck!

The kayaks slid down the whale's back as he rose, twisting in the air and crashing back down, signaling his mate.

-- *Suzette Bishop*

allergy alert
springing from pods of pollen
ready for release

        -- Jane Blanchard

Two Hawks

And seven vultures
Circle in a thermal
Pup proudly displays
 Murdered chipmunk
It took him all summer
To dig out of the woodpile

-- Larry Blazek

Migration

After the courtship
When your scent becomes mine

Let me fold my wings into yours.
Back to back, our union will be complete

And you will lay our seed
Gently upon the milkweed.

Compass to the sun
I promise to keep you near

As we soar south
Three thousand miles

Through field and forest
Until we can rest close and still

And silent, all winter long
in the high pines of Mexico.

-- Irene Bloom

Lost and Found

-- after the great wave of 2011

After floating through all the seasons of the year-
if you can say there are seasons
 out in the wide Pacific - I finally came to rest.

Riding those great wild swells,
many sea creatures
were attracted to me.

While still a bright yellow,
before I faded from the elements,
a huge bluefin thought I was a tasty catch.

But it soon spat me out leaving another
tear in my once crisp brim.
As if I were a plaything, a dolphin

threw me up into the air with its bottlenose,
leaving a huge hole where a perfect eyelet
had been punched into my side.

At last, I lay there battered and bruised
on that foreign beach in Oregon
until a young boy noticed me in the tide pool.

Pockets bulging, he'd collected all sorts of treasures
smooth worn stones, bits of colored glass, spiral shells
like Yuki might have.

When the boy brought me home,
his mother noticed the label inside
with Yuki's name and his school emblem.

Mothers have a way of noticing these things.
She sent me home to Sendai
to my own boy's mother

who wept when she opened
the plain brown envelope.

-- Irene Bloom

Window

the trees
        naked   in the passing winter
               are clothed   in their best spring greenery
no leaf
        torn by hail   or curled to hide an egg
               a breeze touches the understory   skips from tree to tree
the nuthatch
        hikes up the walnut   slips its bill
               under the bark   for an insect hiding from the cold
a chickadee
        flits back and forth   from the feeder
               pounds   the sunflower seed open
the redbud
        shows its magenta dress   to introduce the spring
               the warbler lingers   on the branch to catch
an early gnat
        summer leaves tremble   in the wind that precedes
               the storm   shudder from drops that pummel them
yellow-billed cuckoo
        slinks through the canopy leaves tire
               sourwood reddens   green poplar fades into yellow

the morning light
        outlines the downy woodpecker hitching up the sycamore's trunk

        the trees sulk under a pewter sky

        -- Barbara Brooks

Summer's Turn

humid air
no leaves stir, river flows
sun peeps out

wood pecker
rattles, another answers
a pair

dusk
leaves fade to black
insects sing

midnight
moon smiles
tree frog calls

four a.m.
no leaves stir
all are quiet

-- Barbara Brooks

The Season of Death

hung over the fog like skunk juice,
mulberries heavy and thick,
ripening into black, its leaves
browning to the death hues of autumn.
What was left was left,
what remained began to smell,
everywhere an ending for one species
and a feast for another.

We refused what was in front of us,
pushed back from the table full
and never noticed the drought over the mountain—
it did not pertain to where we were,
water deep and easily cleaned,
stores full of themselves:
money meant nothing
when it no longer mattered.

Summer ended before its time,
We watched it drain itself clear,
bided our time like fugitives,
and wandered into the spray.

-- Michael H. Brownstein

Winter's Harvest

Spring came early this year,
the robins arrived in February
and the great mulberry tree
began developing its harvest
before spring thought itself able.
We wondered why so many nests
and so many birds found themselves
in the branches, but it did not matter—
there were enough for all of us
groundhog, squirrel, vole and beetle—
even after the week long rain,
the cold spurt, the great frost,
mulberries everywhere,
enough food for the season
one season too soon.

-- *Michael H. Brownstein*

One Day the Witch of the Winter Gave Gifts to Her Neighbors

a skinny mural in the back forty and a fat robin among the tree stubs:
she built a platform and a tiny house,
added force and stories until it was poetry
and results.

Everyone is a first and everyone has a first,
a growth,
gnomes and mushrooms, fungus and leprosies until everyone is
colored

blue,
the purple of Lake Michigan deep within the darkness of corn husks.

-- Michael H. Brownstein

Winter, Sort Of

The birds fly south
To avoid the air
That has grown teeth
In the absence of the sun

-- Tanya Bryan

Zero

I woke cold
beneath a
wool blanket
and had bad thoughts
about the landlord
the dirty old
and hurried to
put on clothes
then
sat at the computer
to check emails
but
none to check
and I wondered why
no response
to the poems
I sent
out into the snow
and ice
and ten below east coast weather—
did they all
get
the cold shoulder?

-- Wayne F. Burke

Winter is a Dark Room

Winter is a dark room, a locked door.
Key hidden as I fumble, hands groping
over chill damp walls.
Time is fractured. Runs not in a line
but hovers, almost static in forever twilight,
folds back and forth over itself
in dog-day repetition. Occasionally
a crack of light appears at the door's foot.
Hopeful, yellow-gold. I watch it creep.
Inch infinitesimally slowly. Stifle my impatience
that the gap hasn't widened enough
to offer exit.

-- Miki Byrne

The Dance

The winter grasp, strong,
Objects stiffen in the chill,
Soften to spring's tug.

Light motions of spring,
Petals here, grass shoots appear,
Heat opens summer.

The warmest breeze comes,
Greenery and colors bloom,
In a wink, fall hints.

Hues of fall glimmer,
Trees bend to the calling winds,
Winter's response, cold.

-- Janet Rice Carnahan

Post Card Poem to S From Block Island

It's the end of October and
the seasons are changing as we watch.
The wind shifts and you can see
the rain coming in from The Sound,
moving seaward, advancing as black
streaks before the main storm.
        Gusts of wind buckle the trees,
forgotten wash nearly vertical on their
lines.
        Still the geese are flying, heading
South against the wind. You can hear them
once the thunder stops echoing through
the hollows out over the sea.
        A-

-- Alan Catlin

***Listening to Vivaldi's Four Seasons at Outdoor Amphitheatre
as the Sun Goes Down***

Last light filtered
through standing pines,

streaks of burnt
orange recede

into a field of black
sky studded with

high gray clouds;

on stage a solo
violinist describes

the end of Summer
in a rush of musical

notes.

-- Alan Catlin

Seasons in the Cemetery

Spring

Infinite regret thaws
and eases crocuses
into reviving sunshine.
Daffodils wave light
across the cemetery.
You look for the dead
but cannot find them.
You enquire for the dead.
A snowdrop shakes its head,
points gently to the sky
and says, *They went thataway.*

Summer

The butterflies are holding
scripture in their wings.
The graves know they
are old, discarded chrysalises.
Here death has died, the summer says.
Here heal the human wounds
and calm, courageous souls
bathe warmly in the sun of love.
This is the peaceful airport
where souls prepare to leave
the now unneeded world.

Autumn

You notice the berries,
the full red fruitfulness,
brightness, ripeness, freshness,
the power of the wind,
the dancing leaves
scattered by the breeze,

the dancing lives
risen from their knees.
The wind feels in every shadow
in its search for death
but finds none.

Winter

You expect death and lack of life,
But there they are—buds
on December branches.
Spring is working
in the midst of winter,
in the darkest, coldest days.
And life is also working
here in the funerals.
Here in the darkest, coldest sorrow
joy blooms in the cemetery,
The Resurrectory.

-- Aidan Clarke

Flying South

This is the last time
I go on holiday with my mother.
She reckons there's a lost island
in the middle of the sea,
about a thousand miles away,
where it's nice to spend the winter.

Pull the other one.
It's got feathers on.
There's no such thing as sea or islands.
Winter is for fairy tales
and I can't fly that far in one go.

She was having none of that (daft bat),
so here we are flying south.
I'm sick of this (going nowhere fast).

Wow, look at that.
Where's the land gone?
Look at those waves.

Now, here's the island
and I'm landing on the lovely rocks.
How did she know it was there?
Me ma's not as daft as she looks.

I'll have lots of friends of my own age.
We can meet and date,
recreate, procreate and defecate
for months on end
to our heart's content.
We're guano have a great time.

Quick. Must send a postcard.
Weather here,
wish you were fantastic.

-- Aidan Clarke

The Cuckoo Leaves Home

I was born at midnight
in an alien nest
with a savage hunger
and a compulsion to tidy up.

I thought the unhatched eggs were stones.
For me it was spring cleaning.
To the politically correct brigade
it was ethnic cleansing.

Passing starlings
couldn't resist taunting me
for being adopted.

Mocking birds chorused at dawn.
Where's yer mama gone?
Where's yer mama gone?
Far far away.

Local blackbirds came to sing.
He's fat, he's round,
his daddy can't be found.

My foster parents tried their best,
but that nouvelle cuisine
never fills you up.

Hunger
gnawed at my entrails.

I ran away as soon as I could
and got lost in the Great Forest.

Throughout that first spring
I sat on a branch and stammered.

Need you.
Miss you.
Cuckoo.

-- Aidan Clarke

Long Ago Autumn

After all these years,
it's good to see
the fields of Alcira again
with trees full of oranges
catching the evening sun.

I must confess
I've never been to Alcira
nor even glimpsed those trees
through the window
of the Madrid-Valencia express.

Nonetheless,
those fireballs of fruit
flared up one day
with indelible clarity
and left a sleeping memory
of oranges trees I've never seen.

-- Aidan Clarke

For My Friends, While It's Still Chilly

March is not a pastel month.
It breathes in all the history of ice
and tingles, full with the idea of life.
Drawn from the sharpened shush of snow,
it is an issue settled for us,
a frozen note that stirs, speaks on its own.

But clearly walking still sounds fraught with cold,
and sketched out shades can show no more than hints.
So, March is not a pastel mind.
Yet gray earth choices, we have seen, do lead to fledgling springs.
And when we sing, we'll fan our chilly fire to soft-winged golds.

-- Sharon Cote

The Old Well in the Front Yard:

I knew clear blue water caressing channels far below,
children gathering round to throw pebbles.
They'd wait for the shivery plunk that stirred my depths.

I knew the usefulness of old wooden pails and earthen pots,
and shared my own cool, ruffled words
with summer's hot whispers and winter's icy sighs.

Age is change and ages change, they'd say.
I would laugh with the force of my deep springs.

Yet, in my shifted hoary age I am set shallow,
to rest on solid, breathless earth.

But I do stand, though cracked and dry,
and the quiet memories gather round,
felt as clearly as the soft touch of petals
blown from the garden.

-- Sharon Cote

Snow Angel

Ella and Tod were reading in bed and eating chocolate walnut gelato, homemade from his machine. All the machines belonged to Tod in Ella's mind. Frozen custard was the only dessert she fantasized besides cheesecake, graham cracker crust loaded with cream cheese and sour cream browned around the edges. Good with coffee for breakfast. Last night she dreamed she was sitting on the towel that covered the newspaper that covered her dad's ice cream bucket. It was her job to anchor it while he turned the handle. Her butt grew colder and colder.

"Dad, I'm freezing."

"Just a few more minutes."

Suddenly, she was perched on a block of ice tall enough that her feet dangled above the snow. Her lips almost blue, eyelids so heavy she squinted through a crack. White spread as far as she could see. No houses. No trees. She heard a high-pitched trill and wings opened like a fan in front of her. Ella stood, slowly stretching her arms around his neck, feathers prickly with icicles. Her feet lifted with grace.

-- Chella Courington

The Seasons Took All They Had Come For

the spring was new and ripe with promise,
and you insisted i need an adventure and i
quite agreed;
a new life, a new love
everything was exciting in it's promise
we grew like flowers of the grass and magnolias
in trees
and all around us there was a
fragrance—
summer we were warm and hot
passionate and mad
with sunsets
laughter and lemonade
sheer happiness in one another's company
i was content to leave behind my past to rebuild
a future worth loving with you'
every day seemed to hold a new inspiration
for my pen
to scrawl across the page—
autumn was lovely, too,
we fell and tumbled together like leaves
falling apart and together
clinging like
wild animals to the promise of one another;
i was so happy and you were so charming
everything about us seemed so
sincere—
but winter was the one to kill us
silences became common
communication was null and void
i would try to open like
a snowflake,
but you would blow me away with
the wind of your eyes;
until all that became of us was a one-sided

once love that faded into the darkest
icy lagoon centuries ago.

-- Linda M. Crate

Frosty Proposal

spring came
with all her rain and mud
but with the glimmer
of sunshine,
and i know summer will soon be
here with her sunset colored high heels
kicking off worries with a laugh
that will reverberate deep
into my soul,
and no longer shall i fear or worry
of winter
because he will seem so far away;
autumn will dance in
with all her beauty as a warning
i will not heed
because the children of summer have always been
reckless as the sun—
then one day everything i have loved will die
my favorite flowers buried
underneath an icy hand cruel and long lasting,
and he will try to appease me with
lovely white diamonds
but my rage will only burn as he refuses
to disappear
i could never accept such a frosty
proposal.

-- Linda M. Crate

Burning Frost, Happy Day!

After the bay iced over from Providence to Newport, and the people had walked it that far (or so the press reported), he got a notion he could beat that.

He'd verified the salt and wind in his veins. Friends said he could sail any boat, anywhere, anytime. So later, when a thaw set in and open water began to pock the floating fields of ice, he put on waders and fished out a paddle. Then he boarded an ice slab roughly the shape of a valentine and the size of a floatplane and set off across the west passage between the island and the mainland.

His heart fluttered as he cast off, and he recalled old Eliot saying he had a shine upon him whenever he took the helm. "Must be the Irish red," he said.

But when the wind shifted and the ice proved unruly, he turned himself around and beat the berg back to shore, the oversized heart reduced to the size of a charm by the time he beached.

At home, his mother told him someone had called the local radio to say they saw a boy on an iceberg, paddling across the bay, heading for Plum Point or maybe Wickford. They could not be sure.

"Did you see anybody else down at the beach, dear?" his mother asked.

"No mom, no one."

When his father returned from the fire station, he reported that he'd received a call about boy in the bay, paddling a chunk of ice half way to Wickford.

"The guy called from the bridge, see? And from where he was, he thought he could see red hair on a little guy around your size."

Halfway to Wickford? he thought. Me? That would be the berries. Legendary berries.

"We sent old Eliot down to check," his father continued. "Said he didn't see nuthin' but white caps out there. I'm asking you now, son, was there nuthin' at all to see?"

"What?"

"On the beach, in the water. Was there nuthin to see?" his father persisted.

He shook his head to signal NO, and while his face continued to lie to his father, he imagined people coming from every corner of the island. They came in throngs, raising torches, raising glasses, raising him high and carrying him back to shore ___ the path they made catching fire and burning bright beneath him before it flamed out and froze over again.

-- Wayne Cresser

Soup

"You can't use too many onions,"
mother says, weeping

over half-moon mounds, soup-ready.
Split peas, ham bone ripe with marrow,

stock replete with memory simmer
in a blackened pot on the back burner.

Glasses fog. She lifts the lid, leans in,
her fine-tuned taste like Julia Child's.

Next she adds sprigs of thyme, a dash
of sage, gusto into bowls-full

slurped on frosty days, each sip
toasty, red-hot, a live coal.

-- Betsey Cullen

The Fall

Well I am a little nervous, I must admit. Here I wait, in this luxurious office serving as anteroom to an ever more imposing boardroom, about to surprise the love of my life with my unexpected presence as she enters. She thinks I am in England, in London, in the cooling Autumn winds, leaves swept up by gusts running through the alleyways in the City, funneled and compressed into short blasts of chaos. London is one of the greenest capitals in the world, I've been told. New York has its Central Park – the large lung breathing life into Manhattan, but London has its Hyde Park, the Hampstead Heath, Regents and Richmond Parks and its millions of plane trees, limes, oaks and larches lining roads and standing in back gardens, taking in the bad air, renewing its vigor with oxygen. The same trees do provide the downfall in Autumn though - whoever romanticized about Autumn leaves was ignoring the brown squelchy rain–sodden mess that coats the pavements of the capital. The leaves fall dead to the ground.

No such problem on the sidewalks here in Lower Manhattan in the Fall. Exchanging the FTSE for the Dow, I look out of the window, high up in the block, almost the tallest in New York I can see the green of Central Park as it gradually is turning to brown. In a moment she will walk through the door. Her eyes will widen with surprise. She will mumble and stumble with her words. I will smile and walk forward and take her in my arms. She knows I am going to propose to her, but not here, not now. Today, I know, will be a momentous day for us both – this day in New York in the early September Fall of 2001.

-- Graham Curtis

Dogwoods in Boston

The blossoms float in mid-air
suspended white perfect petals
rippling in the April breeze
surfing the invisible ocean.
Some think they mark the wounds of Jesus,
four stains of red at each corner,
I am not sure of the theology
but there must be a kind of agony
to forge such beauty.
Then looking deeper,
I notice the dull skinny fingers
that support this grace
a cobweb of branches spun beneath,
the delicate trace of bark flowing backward,
downward to the gray rough trunk
that is narrow
and rooted in the icy black soil
waiting for the sun to be unbound.
Life born new and beautiful
again this year
from the roughest patch of barren Boston ground.

-- Oliver Cutshaw

October

In the windows of October
Autumn stretches wide its wings
The earth winds down
To a season tight caught in a web
So howls a coyote with hollow haunches
Through an orchestra of winter wheat

Somewhere in time
The sun with half-closed eyes
Spins oracles
And clouds with memories
Limp across the skies
To follow winds
Sad in the treetops
Winds with dolorous sighs
Singing their poems to me

-- Susan Dale

September, Glorious Stranger

September, again I did not know you
Appearing, as you did,
murmuring breezes of sweet intimacies
winds whispering gold dust
Then October rising triumphant in bronze glory
against the fate of waning autumn
Winter around the bend
wearing grey and gauze gown
Smelling of death
Riding a chariot of swollen clouds
filled with portents of rain
November, closing off sunrays
Laying to waste September's bounty
But again September,
I forgot
And again you came,
as would a stranger
in the bluest of skies,
Like today
before it meets tomorrow

-- Susan Dale

Autumn 2014 – 1

Mist rising from soy-bean fields
In it, the ghosts of autumn
Quiet, golden children
Coming to carry summer off
To a cradle of long sleep

-- Susan Dale

Summer

Rays and rows of gilt,
Brass bowl dripping with honey,
Golden treasures spread.

-- Lela Marie De La Garza

The Penitent

It is high summer. The Piazza di Solo isn't like a normal Italian Square. Sure, there is an over elaborately decorated church filling one face of it, and there is a café with tables and chairs outside on the sunny side opposite, but there is no fountain and there are no noisy Italians singing and dancing and discussing art or politics or life, on the dusty cobbles. There are no old men playing chess and drinking grappa at the tables in the sparse shade of the almost leafless trees. There are no young girls in flirty skirts watching the boys, nor grown women in sophisticated couture sipping coffees, nor old women in black carrying home their shopping. There are no youths in leather jackets on scooters watching the girls. There are no idle or curious tourists sitting out in the glare of the late morning sun, except for me, drinking an overpriced Peroni and eating a pizza made in Glasgow.

I am watching the square as I have done at this time of day for the past few days. I am watching for the little man in the faded white jacket and not quite matching trousers. He will come out of the heavy black wooden doors on the third side of the square, passing through a smaller oblong of black set into the windowless oval of the main doors. He will pause at the threshold as if momentarily blinded by the light, though, at this time of day, his side of the square is already passing into deep shadow. Then he will walk, hesitantly, uncertainly, towards the florid façade of the church.

He will never reach it though, for his steps, each one kicking up a puff of pale yellow dust, will veer towards the centre of the square, which he will pass across before vanishing into the immense but anonymous building on the fourth side.

As he draws closer to me I can see that he has a worried look upon his face and that he glances, almost fearfully, towards the church, which he has once again, apparently, decided not to enter.

No breath of wind blows through the square, and the trees stand silent, motionless, their browning leaves seeming barely alive, and the sounds of the city do not peek in to see what is going on in this baked, forgotten corner. But the Peroni is good, and the pizza too, and I wonder, if I were not there, would the little man make his daily, faltering crossing of the square at all?

I thought I could guess the reason for his unease, for my tourist map has told me that the building that he has come out of is the Convent of Good Heart. It is a gloomy looking place, with no windows upon the ground floor, and with those on the several floors above the level of the oval doors having the blank monotony of a barracks block. Each slab-like window has been covered with what looked like a screen of dark tinted perspex, opaque, but not reflective, and pitted and scarred by the hot, dry, dusty air.

Perhaps, I reason, they had been added to protect the nuns from the sight of the venal, secular life of the square below, in more boisterous times. Now, I reason, by virtue of their small and nervous visitor, perhaps there is more life behind those windows than there was beneath them. On this last morning of my stay I ask the waiter, who speaks very good English, how the man gets away with it?

Gets away with what?

Getting into the nunnery, I explain. He obviously feels guilty about it, but can't bring himself to go into the church and confess, but creeps home, unforgiven!

The waiter laughs.

But it is no longer a nunnery, he says. It is the prison. Marco is serving a life sentence, for murdering his mother. Each day the Governor gives him an errand, to the offices of the Ministry of Justice. He pointed to the anonymous building. He hopes that one day, as he crosses the square, he will enter the church and make confession for his crime.

-- Brindley Hallam Dennis

Seasons Passed

Beneath the dead-fall of autumn
moldering under the melted snow of winter
lay a single rusting brass key,
without fob or ring, just a key—
A copy, you could tell by the markings,
no description or brand name
to identify what the lone key might unlock.

Caught in a rake tine, it roughly scraped,
dragged from the brown-edged lawn onto
pavement, causing me to glance down
at the sound—I lifted the rake to my gloved hand.
Plucking the key loose, I dropped it into
the pocket of my denim jacket and resumed
gathering old wet leaves and decayed twigs
into a pile, a myriad of dull winter saturated debris,
forgotten leaves past the glory of vibrant reds.

The huge maple leaves lay in a sad heap, no memory
of brilliant gold; I listened to the raspy strokes
of the rake on the pavement's edge, uncovering
strange silhouetted shapes, staining the spring walk
in odd patterns, Rorschach-like on the cement canvas.
My hand went unconsciously to the key in my pocket,
the rake forgotten, remembering seasons passed.

-- Julie A. Dickson

The End of Summer

I found summer near death
crawling on the sidewalk;
it had fallen from the trees
and from prehistory. I picked it
up for a closer look: summer
could have passed for an art nouveau
brooch: its Tiffany wings were folded
on an emerald body, its ruby eyes,
now dulled, were set wide upon a cabochon,
its ivory belly a sign of things to come.
I granted it some dignity, and placed it
back on the bark where it gratefully clung—
August's exhausted rattler.

I'm listening to the applause of
crickets now—so many ticket holders
demanding an encore.

-- Joseph Dorazio

October's Retro Gaze

Caught in October's retro gaze
we clash with our own tonalities.
The sea grieves in vast clichés.
Bermuda rides out a hurricane
as if taming a bronco. We pose
before an innocent surf scene
and pretend that the tourist world
has absolved us of our sins against
the restless flux of capital.

We're not actually by the sea,
but this yellow marsh grass waving
in the various light reminds me
that once this entire landscape
relaxed underwater, details
yet to evolve. We could reclaim
to undersea life if we summon
the music of surf to explain
why we look so simple
in our gardening clothes, our fungal
and unruly haircuts glistening.

Better revert to the mud-bottom
where the simple honors itself
with survival or failure to thrive.
Scissoring down the perennials
frostbitten by secretive dark
I feel so raw and exposed
the first shark to come along
could shovel me into its maw
with no show of resistance.

You wouldn't go so easily—
you'd bristle and retort in kind.
You'd mock the predatory instinct
and cast such a gloomy shadow

the shark would realize the sea
drained eons ago, leaving it gasping
in drought of pre-biblical myth.

-- William Doreski

Gloomy Winter Pools

Gloomy winter pools form
in hemlock forest when melt
stalls between seasons. Rimmed

with snow, these pools suggest
evil claw-footed bathtubs
that overflowed centuries ago,

drowning their inhabitants.
I don't know why these pools form
at the highest point of the trail,

where the ridge line angles south
to suggest a view of Monadnock
the dense forest censors. Alone

with the drip of halfhearted thaw
I'm following muddy boot prints
and paw tracks where dog walkers

have passed; but they could be spoor
of a patrol in the highlands near
the Laos border where ambush

scattered bones for tigers to gnaw
weeks after radio contact failed.
The distance the short way around

the globe hardly matters. The shade
of mud is similar, and the glut
of animal hunger lingers

in the wag of family dog.
No ghosts rise from the pool to claim
their memories. I splash through,

embossing new prints and scaring
protozoa forming colonies
on the filthy slick. The hard

arsenic-gray light falters
as the afternoon drags its carcass
to the pool to drink as deeply

as it dares. I trek along sighing
for the dead I'm sure remain dead.
So I add my boot prints to the stock

of clues no one will follow
for fear of discovering more crimes
than brief winter days allow.

-- William Doreski

The Dead of Winter

Behind the convenience store
two guys duke it out. Their fists
windmill the dull winter light,
drawing blood. Their faces knot
into wooden expressions their wives
wouldn't recognize. I phone the cops
to prevent some fatal gesture,
but the voice of a long-dead lover

answers, and I drift a hundred miles
into northern Vermont where skis
hissed across the undulant slopes
and cars skidded, crashed and killed
without remorse or even regret.
That winter smacked of salt and blood.
Hunters dragged carcasses to weigh
at the local general store.

Drug-addled students abandoned
expensive textbooks in snowdrifts.
The scenery wobbled and sometimes
collapsed like a flimsy stage set.
Behind it, vacuums devoid of stars
absorbed the flimsy intellects
of almost everyone I knew
in that generally wide-eyed region.

Now these guys with their foolish
but sincere fist-fight have invoked
the dead of that long-lost winter.
The cops arrive, break it up, and prod
the tough old men into shaking hands.
As the patrol car prattles off,
driving them home, I'm standing
beside a frozen lake at night.

Someone with a flashlight crosses
on foot, the ice groaning. A hand
reaches through the ice and waves,
but the figure with the flashlight
doesn't notice. She reaches shore
with her long hair streaming about her,
and her flatfish gaze affixes me
as I grope for one saving word.

-- William Doreski

Heat

When we can no longer plough our way through it
And it presses and blunts our days and nights

The air conditioner groan their way up the cellar stairs
Like the ghosts of summers past ready to fit again

Once more we close ourselves in like this, windows
And doors shut; we become shut-ins for the season,

Trap ourselves in the heat and then refrigerate ourselves
Part of the way back, someplace in the seventies we feel

A bit better, pretend that the rattle and whir of machine
Made air is also great and will suffice; without real wind

To rend it open we cut the heat apart as best we can – air
Conditioners offering us points of pears and rounds of grapes.

                    -- J.K. Durick

71 Sermons

The uneven languages—
Spoken, written, in frail Braille
Scream broken dead promises,
Where gathering green turns blue
In pale winter, smoldering
Spring wakes, popping frozen worlds,
Cutting love madly into
Two little lost grievances,
The summer kiss is long gone
Leaving skeletons to fall
Alone.

-- Leixyl Kaye Emmerson

Wheat

There is a girl sleeping outside
In a wheat filled yard
And her bed is made of straw
And the trees are swaying in the soft warm
Breeze of the summer
In this glorious evening
In Italy

-- Zach Fechter

Anticipation at Lake Overlook

As I, keeping a promise that I made,
pedal slowly through the curve at Spring Path's Bend,
the chartreuse green and muted yellow blades
sway in the wind. Crimson blossoms send
their fragrance to fluttering butterflies
and bees. Finally lakeside I take a seat,
stare breathless at the skies and then arise
to diamonds flashing on wavelets,
the only gator a word on a sign.
A raft of ducklings separates, unbinds
each to its own society of one.
A splash in the reeds and one shrill call is gone.
Under the live oak limb I'm lost in shade.
Even the bird above is not afraid.

-- Sharon Fedor

Snow Maiden

The home office really does have it perks. I climb out of bed and immediately check my phone for any late night messages. I can hear my son moving around in his room, getting ready. Proud of him for taking initiative without my aid.

Downstairs I prepare the breakfast and lunches for my two men so they can get moving when they head downstairs. Fred will take Tony to school and then head over to the office so that gives me the time I need to look at my schedule. I unlock my computer and check my various email accounts to see what information I'll need for the current project, named Four Seasons. My employer is always prepared and has sent me an email with the necessary photos, schedules and video feeds that I need to make sure we have everything in order. Phone vibrates and I realize I missed a call last night while I was sleeping. I type in the password and listen to my employer dictate instructions, letting me know the timetable for our project has been moved up by HQ. They need phase 1 completed today which means my day just got a hell of a lot busier. I know what I signed up for but there's no question how difficult this makes things. I thought I had more time.

I ran back to the kitchen quickly before my conference call at noon and see that Fred left a note on the fridge.

"Hon, got that big meeting today. Probably won't be home for dinner so don't wait up. Talked to my Mom, she'll take Tony after school. Love you lots."

My heart smiles as I bring the note close to my chest. Our marriage is still young but the love we share is real. I need him to always believe that. Deep breaths and *focus* before I sit down in my chair and get ready for the call. Appearing weak is always bad for business. In my line of employment we get new employees every couple weeks and I'm responsible for them. They don't get any 'training', that's done way before they get to me. We all get on the line, some have worked with each other before on different projects but no pleasantries are exchanged.

"Did you receive my email Winter?"

"Of course," I said. "The video surveillance looks pretty solid. Spring on the inside will make sure that's the only room available for booking. Our research tells us that there will be five men and two women in the room when our project will commence."

Man number two who identifies himself as Summer speaks, "I reviewed the schedules you sent me this morning and I'll be on the floor while the meeting is taking place. Photos were taken at JFK earlier this week upon Director Cross's arrival. I've confirmed with his chauffeur that he intends to be at the meeting with some security. We have Spring suited up as part of his detail."

Another male voice speaks up, codename Fall, "How you get that info Summer? *Deep* undercover?"

I interrupt, "Gentlemen, remember this is a business call so please cut the crap for now. Can everyone confirm that the situation is green lighted and we have all pieces in motion for success. Confirmed?"

Four yeses and I terminate the call. I haven't gotten where I am today by letting men walk all over me. Some curse me, I say it's proper planning for my future.

The email comes in confirming my flight to Paris in a few hours. I quickly pack a bag and reach for my phone. The thought of Tony creeps into my head. He'll be so confused. I'm quite aware this will be the most difficult call I've ever had to make but I tell myself its necessary and part of something bigger. The call triggers the C4 in my husband's bag, which sits in conference room A between Security Director Cross and the father of my child. Summer confirms mission success with a quick text, Spring didn't make it. A tear tries to force its way from my eye but I quickly dispose of it. The Four Seasons will reconvene in Paris and she knows Winter will need to be cold. Just like it always is.

-- Michael Freveletti

Seasonal Affective Sestina

How is it possible that meteorology isn't a load of bullshit?
Five inches of snow on the first day of spring.
I thought we had passed through the grips of winter.
It's not like when I lived in Upstate New York where it didn't stop being winter
until summer.
Upstate was always more for the lion-hearted except during autumn
With its from apple picking and fall foliage blankets.

Watch this weekend be another one where I'll need the extra blanket.
Someday, I'll finish with that bullshit
By that time, the calendar will have already changed to autumn,
And will have barely remembered when it was spring.
Although, there were those 103 degree days to remember in the summer,
Which had me praying for winter.

When winter
Finally came, it blanketed
The earth with enough snow to spark the wish for summer,
And more of the circular bullshit,
Which shortens the spring,
And steals the grandeur from autumn.

I miss the extended autumnal
Smell of fireplaces and dead leaves, which are a rite of passage to winter.
A season not just containing muskiness but a black blanket
That is as messy as bull's shit.
Mud that can only crack in the baking sun of summer.

What of those miserable days of summer,
When that stranger on the bus when I was in Boston eulogized autumn.
Chalking another death up to climate change. "This bullshit
Has got to stop," he complained. "The bastards are coming for winter."
By bastards, I think he meant oil companies blanketing
Congress with money while they attended Easter egg hunts each spring.

I'll delight in the melancholy of early spring.
I'll dutifully go to the beach in the summer.
I'll know in the end the price of a good blanket,

102

And I'll keep it in the cedar chest 'til autumn.
But I'll never forgive an unending winter
Or Staten Island Chuck's bullshit.

Under my blanket, until the autumn, sleeping through spring
Revealing in the summer's march toward winter's bullshit.

-- John Gallagher

First Flush

Mountains flush with dawn frost
   blossoms of magenta
   then scarlet, crimson lake
chlorophyll not yet overwhelming first leaflets

-- Susan Gardner

Digging Potatoes in August

Mid-day, through the opened door,
I see his pallid face. He checks the clock,
without a word, turns over,
pulls the blanket up. I swallow hard,
tiptoe downstairs, leave the house,
then brave the August glare
to go into the garden.

Dark eruptions, tell-tale mounds,
akin the spots which mar his skin,
rose over night,
a gopher's tailings.
I want to beat it
before it can devour
what I claim to be mine.

I fetch the spading fork and dig
golden orbs from gray, dried-out soil.
I fill two buckets, straighten my back
as I lift my load and, passing, glance
at the teardrop-shaped patch
of prickly thistles pushing up
through the mulch.

-- Brigitte Goetze

Bad Weather

This is my first venture out.
I sit in the car.
I feel the heat of the sun on my dashboard.
Sunny and seventy five degrees;
bad news for me.
I have blockaded myself indoors for days
with broth and tea.
Now, a drive to my local pharmacy.
I could decide not to go straight home,
instead, loop around the park,
see the buds and blossoms, unfurling leaves,
fresh new green.
I wish I were restored
and felt, as in summer,
the impetus to just keep going, to drive South.

-- Elissa Gordon

How to Plant a Tribute Garden

Forget a formal plan
and serious intent.
Seek a graceful stalk
that recalls her silhouette.
Draw on colors from their wardrobe, their home,
borrow from favorite parks and gardens
in travels of your own.
Don't wear gloves! (Roses aside)
Feel the earth, smell the soil,
even if it is hanging baskets and window boxes,
with each seed and seedling
envision planting her energy.
Keep a favorite photo of the beloved nearby,
you don't have to go solely from memory.
Put on a pretty dress.
At a local nursery or garden center,
stroll, laugh, linger,
among all the colors and fragrance,
the flamboyant, the muted and dusky.
Chat with the young men buying plants
for their mothers.
Hand them a fuchsia.
Say, *she will love this,*
it blooms over and over
all spring and summer.
Return home, arrange, rearrange and plant,
taking in the dewy blooms, the open sky,
the faint rustling of new leaves, the tender air.
Reminisce out loud, gesturing toward the place next to you
empty like Elijah's chair.
Sigh with longing and nostalgia at the closing of this day
You'll have to deadhead those flowers in two weeks
you can almost hear her say.

-- Elissa Gordon

A Perfectly Good Day

I did not go outside today.
There was a chill in the air,
colors shook in the wind
like papers rustling,
a little restless, a little reckless,
a quintessential autumn day.

At 5:54 as the skies darkened
I regretted it,
the day spent folding and stacking
sweaters and shirts, scarves,
gear for winter treks,
I logged each movement and then
wanted to lock forever in time
the luxury of a solitary life.

-- Elissa Gordon

Coastal Winter

In this weather you have
only thoughts wrapped around you,
hold up a hand and you
see no shadow nor do
you see yourself in sand;

kick the icy chunks
along the lifeless shore
--except sea birds living in
another dimension
moving at unfathomed speeds--

no ancient marble blocks,
just poured concrete made
by modern man who
continues to chip away
nature until you stand there
alone and bare.

-- Ray Greenblatt

7°

This is an unknown zone.

Autos droop fangs of ice,
church bells ring sharper tones,
sidewalks slant with frost,
toes send dull signals.

Do not trust trains with signs
that state: Rails may be
slippery in autumn,
frozen switches in winter.

I keep meeting drafts
like malevolent
phantoms from the past.
Snailing down side-streets

I grow envious
of puffing chimneys.
Dunkin Donuts a line-shack
on the lower forty.

-- Ray Greenblatt

A Warm Day in February

It is a day much too warm
for what the calendar tells me.
Winter takes the time off.
Spring doesn't show its colors,
but highlights where
they'll be coming from.

Snow melts away like magic.
The forest is fooled.
Hibernations snap suddenly.
A handful of golfers
stride expectantly onto the course.

No wind.
No clouds.
The sun even feels like it's working.
Kids rummage through dresser drawers
for tee-shirts.
Older couples walk
when a week before,
they slid.
A park bench is occupied once more
by the memories of ancient soldiers.

Forecasters are predicting
temperatures lower than normal
for tomorrow,
maybe six inches of snow by afternoon.

But today is out of the forecaster's hands.
It's happening
and for the better.
My body takes up

where last summer left off.
My mind is befuddled
but fine with it.

-- John Grey

Last Snowflake in Spring

If it knew how long it would last
on the ground
it wouldn't even bother
to fall.

The sun is following close behind it.
The temperatures are rising.
It alights on a leaf,
the burgeoning petal of a flower,
for the briefest of times,
reminds the greenness
all around it
that there will be other winters.

But it will melt
before it is believed.

-- John Grey

Fall

Brittle fragments, little, shredded, crispy bits of skin
drained of chlorophyll, dead
brittle cast offs. The silver maple
shudders in the November wind
and discards the tips of its body, its plugs
into the passion, the ebb and flow of the universe.
Here it stands now, empty torso
graying in sunlight. Thick bark
cracks and slivers but holds firm
against the loss and dark
of winter's bitter angst. The buds
of next spring line themselves
up on twigs and twists of branches.
They wait. The tree waits. The wind
rails forth and the sun comes and goes,
but the tree waits, its roots
growing the whole length of an earthworm's burrow, and
deeper.

-- Pat Hanahoe-Dosch

Detritus

The army of gold leaves rolled and hopped across the grass
of the cemetery. A few clung to gravestones, set up camp
in the crease between the dirt and stone. Others drifted
quietly away from the horde, tried to fly back to the tree
that launched their light, brittle bodies into the wind.
Most scattered when they felt the road under their crackling tips.
The entire world was open to them if they could float or roll long enough.
But not before their skin tore and broke down
into shredded filaments of golden light, and mulched
the ground around the dead, joined the merry mass
of molecules humming all around the ground hogs' burrows and tunnels
that weave between cement vaults buried in thick mud.

-- Pat Hanahoe-Dosch

Between Seasons

". . . there's only four seasons, and I'm looking for something more."

-- Joe Purdy

It's the time of year when we
No longer hear the whoosh
Of the gas burner lighting off
Or the slow crescendo of the furnace fan.
The thermostat is set neither
On heat nor cool as air handlers
And compressors fall silent
As an old mans' unused tools.
And when we open all the windows,
It only takes a few hours for the house
To smell fresh again after a long winter.
It is a short season between seasons
When the house becomes
One with the natural world.
At night, crickets and frogs play
Their fiddles outside in the darkness.
A moth plastered onto the window screen
Basks in faint incandescent light
From an old Tiffany lamp on an oak table.
Mosquitoes still slumber while we have
Cold drinks unbothered on the front porch.
But the intermission between seasons
Is short even though we wish it were longer.
When summer creeps up with her aura
Of insects, heat and humidity,
We reluctantly close each sash
As if sealing an air lock before a dive
To the bottom of the ocean.
And then the fan clicks on pushing
Frigid air through ductwork and fiberglass filters

116

To preserve us until the end of summer,
When for a brief time, we can open
All the windows once again.

-- William Ogden Haynes

What's Beautiful Anyway?

I'd asked him, "Am I beautiful?" I wasn't looking for honesty, just a stroke of my ego, but he hesitated a second too long.

"Beautiful enough for me." He murmured. What did that mean? So I was in a bad mood when I set off for the concert. He offered to take me. Another mistake!

"I'm blind – not stupid"' I snapped, as my cane nosed out of the door and along to the bus stop. I flashed my pass at the driver and went to the front seat. Somebody moved out of my way and I mumbled my thanks. I'd loaded the four allegro movements of the Vivaldi into my player. That always lasted for the journey. It began with the Winter movement. I loved that, with the sparkling pizzicato notes sounding like snowflakes. My mood lifted with it. I'd been too grumpy with him. Did it matter whether I'm beautiful or not? Somebody rang the bell to get off at the library.

Most people like the Spring movement best, with its suggestion of birdsong and flowers. It's not my favorite but I was enjoying the simple melodies as the bus turned sharp left at the roundabout, forcing me to my right. I was looking forward to the concert. I'd been chosen to sing the solo and I'd been practicing for ages. I asked my friend Lizzie why she thought I'd been chosen and she laughed and said that the choirmaster liked novelty and a little blind soprano fitted the bill this year. She'd been the solo last year so I asked what was so damned unusual about her. She said it was because she's black and I said, Oh – are you? That made her howl with laughter. Well! How was I to know? Anybody can look at me but I have to ask permission to look at you. Anyway, I had a good look at her and she didn't look any different from me. Her hair was a bit crispy, that's all.

The bus slowed as we moved into the traffic in town just as Summer began. You'd think this would be all soft and sultry but the thunderstorm element is really dramatic. People began to shuffle down the bus as it stopped every minute or so. I was going into the bus station so I stayed put. Somebody said Excuse Me in that enunciated way as if I'm deaf as well as blind. I hadn't realized she was sitting

118

next to me by the window. I moved my knees out of the way and she eased past.

As we trundled through town my favorite movement began. I love the Autumn movement with its images of singing and dancing as the peasants celebrate the harvest. That's how I see it anyway. Perhaps that's why I love music so much. I can see it just as clearly as sighted people can. I ran my hands through my hair, hoping I was tidy for the concert. Lizzie would be there though, and she'd put me right. The music finished as the bus pulled into the bay and I took my headphones off. I smiled. I'd had a lovely journey through the Four Seasons. Lizzie was waiting for me and we walked arm in arm to the concert hall.

I changed into a silk dress that caressed me when I moved and I wriggled slightly to enjoy the sensation. Lizzie sat beside me on the platform as we waited for the conductor to arrive. Mine was the first item on the program. After the applause for the conductor had died down, the audience settled into that buzz of shuffling and whispering that passed for silence. Lizzie patted my hand.

"Head up, hands by your sides and don't swivel your eyes around. It makes you look weird."

So I was smiling as I stood up. The notes of the Ave Maria seemed to rise through my whole body up to the ceiling of the hall. When it was finished there was silence for a heartbeat and then the applause rose and wrapped me in a warm cloak of love. Beautiful!

-- *Eileen Holmes*

January

Along the Embankment,
concealed in river mist,
a regiment of gray ghosts
stared out from their shelters.
Had I anything to give,
I would have, and gladly,
in honor of the kindness of strangers,
and to spare at least one of them
from scavenging the frozen trash
for tonight's sustenance.
But I was following too closely,
my hands hollowed and raw.

-- Ruth Holzer

Unfrozen

While winter claims the earth
The backyard becomes
A maze of crystal covered branches

Would hold tight roots planted within

Leaves frozen in somber sleep now awaken
To new life within the water.
With a responsibility to stand alone
Absent the cowering, the covering of snow

Pine trees bear witness to merciless wind
While bluebells splash onto untamed grass
Geese honk overhead and gray skies part
To expose storms while

The man sheds tears

Water lends relief
As leaves still anchored are not yet
Shed.

-- *Carol Hornak*

The Summer of the Epidemic

Mother scuttles about the kitchen
slathers peanut butter, grape jelly on Wonderbread
slaps sandwiches together like spankings

slices triangles from each white square
arranges them in star shapes on floppy paper plates
for our picnic lunch in the backyard

where we head to sit and sip cherry Kool Aid
from sweating metal tumblers we hold with both hands
and swish to hear the ice cubes clink against the sides

I am nine and watch the black garden hose
fill our green canvas pool with water
that sparkles in the sunlight like sprinkled tears

Mother wears her worry face, not her swimsuit
says we have to wait an hour before we jump in
we whine but her eyes show it's no good to argue

It's to keep you safe, she says
we pout, blow the heads off white dandelions
make a wish on each floating seed wisp

we watch for the scold, a warning about weeds
but Mother's mouth smiles and she joins us
chasing silk strands across the prickly lawn

I know now it's the summer
they think Daddy might have polio

-- *Susan Martell Huebner*

Red Barn

On a day when the sky is padded with clouds,
she rides in the backseat behind her mother and father,
looks out the window and sees the first red barn.
Nestled in a swirl of hill, it reels in her imagination
like a rainbow fish. She hears the soft whinny of
a pony named Nickel, feels the wiggling velvet of
a basket of kittens squirming beneath her hand.
Finally, the cottage at the end of a one-lane road.
She stretches a beach towel over the warm planks
of the pier, digs with pleasure into a brown grocery bag
stuffed with library books, leaves for Rhett Butler,
easily conjured in the smoky puddles that hang in the air
from her father's cigar. Mother calls to lunch; she returns.
For a while, she watches the raft bob and wink an invitation,
but she declines, preferring Merlyn and Wart and dreaming
her future in the sighing trees and lapping waves.
As the week ends, she turns away slowly,
climbs back into the city girl's frame.
Inside a red barn, a pony named Nickel
whinnies goodbye.

-- Susan Martell Huebner

The Promise of Heat

The year is at red berries.
Trees on the ridge swallow fleeing birds
only to release them
in a sudden patterned spurt
like water from the garden hose.

Already stiffening with cold,
the green snake coils reluctantly
as I bed him down among lawn chairs and barbecues.
The serpent sleeps.
Summer slumbers.
Only in berries the promise of heat,
red and radiating.

-- Liz Hufford

Swan Song for Winter

Winter is sloughing off the lawn
Slouching toward the curb she shoulders
Aside pebbles and debris tossed up
By snow removers determined to reach
The gutter before the melting season
Sinks its teeth into her crunchy edges
Tears her asunder, tatters her apart
Makes an end to her too soon, too soon

-- S.E. Ingraham

Lift Bridge

Another beginning, that's Spring in your step, the sun's
complicity as afternoon heat rises & wind teases along,
ruffling a fluid skirt that's swirling with neon tetras dis-

appearing below the knees & the gaze of a young man is
your amusement as he watches you feeling utterly alive,
crossing the lift bridge— chin up—five bells ringing.

-- M.J. Iuppa

The Way Home

Show me the balloon tire bike with its red leather seat
left akimbo in the yard, one wheel up still spinning
with its clothespin's clipped-click of a one-eyed Jack
counting the spoke seconds before the sun goes down.

Breathless & sunburned, finding the utter quiet in
our cottage where my father reads beneath a lamp,
hardly raising his eyes to check his watch, he nods
at me, affirming one second left before moonlight.

And, in that moment of race, I try to contain my
thrill that rinses over me in a shudder, knowing
I shaved another second off my best time, and
I could fly— I could fly— all the way, home.

-- M.J. Iuppa

The Seasons in 4 Cinquains

Wild winter wind . . .

so loud
moves down the street.
Touches, trashes, ices.
I run home. Against its cold push
door closed.

A Perfect Moon

And now,
it's the last day
of winter. Spring is here.
They say it's a good night for moon
watching.

Summer's Blink

The sun
is out. And soon
it's gray. Rain comes as if
crystal eyelashes. View's sun-filled
again.

Glory of Color

It's fall.
Leaves will be missed.
They'll be littering paths.
I'll try to look for positive
changes.

-- Evie Ivy

Still the Year Turns . . .

waterfall unlocks
the icy bands of winter
river flows away

daffodil trumpets
herald signs of coming Spring
blossom on the bough

chattering swallows
huddled on the humming wire
summer daylight fades

mournful cries at dusk
dark wings in the red streaked sky
wild geese flying south

-- Diane Jackman

Winter Sequence

cold air   colder air
varying temperatures
air in city square settles
warming slightly

moderate sun   air rises
first flakes
cold blows in

forecast of change
heated buildings
snowflakes tumble
settle on ledges
streets gather strewn flakes

night settles a whiteness
snowflakes attach to roofs
branches turn white
moon sheds a yellowness

morning light on river's frozen edge
boats lights reflect blue
the thames catches some sky
wrapped figures mull past

streets change form
faces at windows
children skid in the park
build a snowman

soft lights in city blocks
some windows dark
flakes increase

a figure crosses the square
moving umbrellas change shape
the shoeless man shelters under an arch

-- Juli Jana

Summer Street

houses that were once blank open their walls
jerry finds his feet   the old man next door dies

jane her husband & son live together for one week
caroline is looking for the man of her dreams

waits at the gate every evening with birdsong
the socialite welcomes judges and buskers

adam swears & twitches non-stop
a professor places tulips in the window

norbert lives alone with his cough
a polish family house a second family

crowd bicycles onto their balcony
sam writes songs & sitcoms

the gardener plants cabbages for butterflies
in the basement an artist paints circles

-- Juli Jana

I Had Always Wondered About Knots in Trees in Spring

in winter saw the same ones today van gogh painted
bulging knot upon knot hardened
cut to size year upon year

                                            stumps at eye level
dark after snow and ice

                                               rootlike branches thin
straight spread out

this morning new greenness
each shoot - shimmers

                                        catches
light thrown back and forth
ducks fly past squawking in protest

                                        head
along canals and polders

I turn to vincent telling him   the potato planters are missing
                                    the water nearly floods the banks
                                    not quite for the bogs still drain

the windmill harnesses a light breeze
its reflection shocked into the whole of a passing cloud
the farmers dry hay in the sheds
cows on polders lift heads slowly
smell the vapour rising with the sun
sense this day is the same as last spring
and the time before

an accumulation of many mornings
the smell deepening spreads the distance

                    -- Juli Jana

April Winds

April winds persist
in doing charity work
early through
willow tree branches
melting reminisces of
snow crystals
on my balcony.
Canadian geese wait
impatiently for their
winter feeding below.
The silent sounds
they hear –
no dropping
of the sunflower
seeds.

-- Michael Lee Johnson

Even as Evening

Even as evening
approaches night-
green dandelion leaves
shake dust from their yellow flowers.
A stray robin pulls up the last
red worm from
a rotting corncob.
Earth is turning callous–
shadows fade flake off
into fresh fall night-
small creatures
with trumpet
sounds dominant
the adjacent
woods.
A virtuoso!

-- Michael Lee Johnson

Fall is Golden

The last golden yellow apple
hangs like a healing miracle
bow down old apple tree
winter is coming.
Life is a single thread this time.

-- Michael Lee Johnson

My Caribbean

Outside, old snow caked into ice,
cold so bitter it tightens the spaces
between your teeth.

Inside, an expanse of turquoise
where swimmers ply their laps, the rhythmic slap
of arms, fluttering feet kicking up splashes.

Water temp: 84 degrees, warmer than the outdoor pool
in summer. Warmer than Bermuda in February,
than New England's arctic embrace.

No diving allowed, I enter the pool backwards
like climbing down the ladder on a boat
into another world, another freedom.

The first strokes are the best.
Lungs filled, I strike out for the deep end,
my arms reaching, palming the water, moving it back

as my body stretches forward.
Lighter than a leaf spinning to the ground,
than a finger-tip on an infant's cheek,

and fast, not as a Harley racing,
but an arrow reaching its mark, my head leading
the way in its tight silver cap.

Shoulders and hips moving as one,
I am Diana Naiad subduing waves from Cuba
to Key West.   The edge touched,

I flip on my back, one arm lifted over my head
then back down into the water.   Eagerly, its twin follows.
My Caribbean, I embrace you.

-- Claire Keyes

Come September

Cars and trucks ascend our dirt road.
It's rough, the driving slow and noisy: rocks
crunch, engines strain. Gun shots in the distance,
perhaps a rifle or a shot-gun. Some days
it's just our neighbor with his automatic weapon.
He likes to practice on weekends, spraying the cornfield.
Soft-nosed alpacas, grazing within their corral,
stampede towards the barn as if he were aiming for them,
but he has no plan in mind, just the pleasure of firing his gun.

Between blasts, the air is translucent, the only sound
the twitter of chickadees, those friendly souls,
pursuing hunters through the woods. I've seen them
perch on a hand if one were proffered.
Hunters move along, barely making a peep.
Ruffed grouse is their pleasure, groundlings
they flush from the underbrush, a flurry of wings
and anxious piping. Autumn woods light up for hunters.
Accurate, deadly, they blast it right back.

-- Claire Keyes

Molly

Late summer and starlings descend on drenched lawns.
The neighborhood hums with their excitement.

Earthworms, after pounding rain, have been known to emerge
onto wet grass and starlings whoosh past porches

and cover the lawn like scattered checkers.

There's something more, something better---over there,
and soon the tall trees shiver with their presence.

Is it always like this? The promise of feast, the feeding frenzy.
Like the bluefish following the silversides close to shore, the beach
ruffling

with their pleasure, so many appetites, so much glut.
At clubs in the city, college girls overdose on *molly*, a more refined

ecstasy, seeking its embrace of warmth and intimacy.
Good girls from the suburbs with great GPAs

having a night out, nothing bad can happen to them,
not with so much pleasure to be had.   One dies, then another:

concert deaths they call them.
Smart white girls too dumb to say no. Girls like me.

Another age, another time: alcohol my drug.
Until all I remember is lying on a couch being groped

by several men, then "Moon" Mullins with his roguish smile,
took over and I don't know what prevented the rape.

Perhaps some shred of dignity left in my body or even some restraint
on his part not to devour the drunken virgin that night.

It's never not like this, appetites building, even raging.
My brother, home from the war, a man now and deserving

his beer cold from the fridge. Only we are teetotalers
and swifter than any grown son can pop his brew,

my father flings the six-pack into a snow bank.

A few bottles rest amazingly intact until rescued by my brother
whose defiance will roam into the town's tap rooms and vets' clubs---

but not the VFW where my father, the Commander, presides.

So I never learned to drink, never sipped a little wine at a holiday table
or understood the difference between 100 proof vodka and a beer.

I watch the starlings on my lawn, the flock taking over,
signals passed back and forth, the energy

funneling through the bodies, their beaks probing the damp earth
until one lifts off then another

amid much chirping, sending signals to one another. There's something more,
something better, over there.

-- Claire Keyes

Summer and You

If I forget
the way time swooped
around you like crocodile
shoes flapping on a beach.

If I forget
your waves crashing against
the rocks, fast and slow.

If I forget
your fishing boats like
beads on a chain, the crunch
of granite under my feet, the
white owls, the wheeling gulls.

If I forget you,
will you come and get me?

-- Lori Kiefer

Autumn Returns

Copper leaves crunch,
crisp around my feet.

The night returns,
burnt from the sun.

The sky crumbles,
time contracts,

feather birds fly
over forest and gulch.

Memories of you
turning to mulch.

-- Lori Kiefer

Wind chasing snowflakes,
swirling on pavements.
Soon they will be blossoms.

-- Lori Kiefer

The Spring Curmudgeon Realizes What Comes Next

Spring, a hussy with pendulous wisteria plumage,
a burlesque queen dipped in the scent of star jasmine.
Spring, a chorus line of leg-lifting bee-attracting blooms,
kicking to the screeches of lusty crows and blue jays.

The mania jacks up my immune system
until I feel as if one of those bees had just stung me,
it's fuzzy body so strung out on pollen
it mistook my scrawny neck for a threat.

Spring, when it's time to go out in the park, hike a trail,
bring some tissues and an inhaler, punish my lungs
with the gorgeous pollen-infested air.

Just get over it! Spring over all barriers. Find the tulips
in their vase dropping petals like strippers.
They're beautiful. And it's not so bad to stay inside.
Oh yes it is! Who am I kidding? So here I am,
the violence of a season at my shoulder,
heat and sunshine waiting with their frying pan and anvil.

-- Phyllis Klein

The Summer I Was Ten

I swam across Fairview Lake early one morning,
while wisps of fog floated just above and bullfrogs

twanged their parting songs, invisible among trees.
I made for the point, skinny arms flashing,

hands cupped, legs kicking, knees locked
and straight, breathing every fourth stroke, a rhythm

to quell whatever wild panic remained in my
mistrustful lungs. At the far shore I walked the last

few yards, muck up to my ankles, nearly slipped
on an algae-coated log and lay down to rest on dew-

soaked grass, rivulets running down my forehead, wet
hair slung back against my neck. In the distance now

brightly colored boats danced gently in their docks
and bold morning gulls swooped on glittering waves.

-- Steve Klepetar

Summer in the Everglades

Water torrents aiming perfectly
in between aged palm trees
like thrown bowling balls
deep in the American Amazon
during summer months

the alligators don't mind
as they comfortably hide under a bridge
waiting until the last raindrops
fall from lichens swinging in harmony
to the sound of the ibises and sandhill cranes

the dried reminders of what faded jasmine blossoms
strewn across a hidden lake surrounded by
a seashell covered trail that crunches underfoot
cleansing a dream in paradise.

-- Julie Kovacs

Through Flames in the New Year's Fire

Winter, Last

Between the hydrangea and forsythia,
bare limbs snagged remnant spider strands
beaded with raindrops.

There were accidents. That gramma in the emergency room
believed she was in a pew in church
until she peed in her pants.

Greens – the neon moss backed the synagogue cornerstone steps
to the sanctuary where the folksinger's casket rested on a bier.

An ad in the *New York Times*
announced new zombie books
to ship on Valentine's Day.

Icicles hung like fiendish teeth.

Spring

Snowdrops first.

The ornithologist explained his diagnosis,
his fingers fluttering
over the rose coverlet on his bed.
He said it would rain soon.
It was sleeting.

In the damp cardboard box packed with bone china teacups,
one dry spider curled in yellow newspaper from 1992.

In the barn, piles of shed horse hair
blew into corners of drafty stalls.
Two mice molded in hayloft traps.

Summer

Ripe peach skin
hid the rugged terrain of pits.

To transplant pearly everlasting for the bees,
I tugged apart thick, tangled roots.

The third-grade teacher died from Alzheimer's.
Her daughter set out red candles, red geraniums
and a photo of her best and second marriage.
We heard Navajo flute songs.

Fall

One pencil-thin stem of a white rose held on to one brown leaf.
Maple leaves studded the sidewalk with red stars.
I saw no night stars during four weeks of fog.

Professor "Bird Man" died.
I drove 95 miles from a poetry reading
to the century-old red barn for his family's tribute,
wearing the same gray-and-black-striped dress to both.

Tacked to the wall of the barn –
a dusty red second-place ribbon
from a horseshow in 1998.

Winter, This

The forecast shouts out polar vortex.

My fire in logs of compressed wood chips
sputters on the bed of raked ash. I eat
a pomegranate, red food for the dead.

I redeemed a gift certificate at Powell's Books.
From a poetry shelf, side by side
nested birth, love, aging and death. I chose Bly.

I drink an aged Brunello.
My fingers massage the gutter of the book.
I touch words nearby, *prepared for death.*

-- Tricia Knoll

The Counting of Blessing

for Hoss

what seems unfair
is as perfect as everything else
the astrologer contends as rain begins
its winter incursions
                              her words like
crossing hot scree
with blistered feet
                              like
spikes against the tender
flesh of the soul
                    let go
let god she glares
& he's trying not to scream
screw your truisms
your "there is goodness
in everything"
                              if
poetry is a piercing through
a portal for what
might otherwise not impress the air
must we not invent
a surrender more keen
                              but
despite himself
                    as if
the ramparts of the known
had hauled themselves
free of primeval origin
                              as if gratitude
had already loosed its ontological
toxin
          he leans in

                    later
after the rain
he travels north
                    hills
spill green & gold to the Pacific
glamor of spring
over desert's stoic
constant
          but this is no mere
seasonal ardor
               it's the shoals
of a dialectic that brooks
no equivocation
               & time
is no longer on his side
                    fifty
                         career
recanted
          his next incarnation
as elusive as the blessing
he is to master
through want

               winter
                    a shiver
as he crossed
the San Joaquin
               soul-cracking
emptiness
          as if
the very concept of nothing
made nothing
inevitable
          & slowly
                    like the first
stars that pressed into evening
above a fading world

something
came
if there is beauty
it lives in the ache
to seek it out

let go
he dares this night
as sleep dissolves all construct
& there is nothing more keen
than silence
summon shadow
summon light
summon every terror I know
& I will submit

morning
opens his eyes yet again
to fingers of rain
beckoning soft & dense
through the jade plant's supplicant
leaves
could this be the countenance
of a new world
& would he
recognize it if it were
as he drifts
upward into himself he knows
sudden & somatic
that these five days have done
more than wash him
clean
they have honed the edge of him
so he can no longer ignore
the weight of what sustains
bamboo

that quivers wind-riven
above his balcony
                    sky in its pure
grey insanely radiant
glory
          the fierce devotion
of his pulse
                    & the astrologer
who at the end closed her eyes
released a ragged breath
wondered *how much miracle
can one fool refuse*

                    -- Kevin Kreiger

Winter Afternoon, Café Strip, Fremantle

The sky darkens, swells, bursts
to release a torrent, a downpour.
Sheets of silver fall earthwards,
plummeting pell-mell into our faces.
We are blinded.
Cars cruise grey streets,
with wipers thrashing out an urgent rhythm;
counterpoint to the drumming rain

Crowds break and run for it
Cramming into the shelter of coffee shops,
or book stores, where
light gleams on wild hair
and droplets cling, loathe to let go.
Coffee smells good in the fuggy warmth
where our mingled breath steams up the windows.

Outside, puddled water
gilds the tarmac with silver.
Like wraiths,
vapors rise and drift on chill air.

-- Veronica Lake

Come to Me

when the wet season, the cyclones
have passed, rainforest trees are lush
the frangipani leaves on the ground
brittle and brown as dust.

Come in the soft April moon,
when the white-bark trunks on the riverbank
glow reddish against the afternoon sky.

Come when the night wind howls off-key
drives the humidity to the horizon's edge
when the ocean starts cooling down
                     half-heartedly.

When you come to me as the rose robin in April
the days will be shorter. We'll have time to read.
We'll harvest and eat berries off the windowsill.

-- Martha Landman

I Never Wanted to Leave

this river park
with its Flamboyant trees
the benches where lovers meet
the knowingness, the surety
of a thousand days in step
around this river

I never wanted to leave
these black cockatoos who prey
like priests on the lawn
their itchy feet
scribbling roadmaps in the sand

I will go far away
walk in Jacaranda cities
be cold in winter
pine for the same sun
that kept Africa warm
and come back
to these mountain clouds
the orange sky at dusk
the turtles forever
feeding on bread crumbs

there's no other way
no other water
I will be back

-- Martha Landman

Of Rain and Skin and Cloud

Your body is summer
your breath salt as the sea, a postscript
infused by moons and stars
there are flames, there is freedom
the world heeds a cry

Touch the moon
fill the hills and valleys with meerkat eyes
sing your song
of rain and skin and cloud

Let the rivers run across your land
your passion drown in bliss
let your days carry the sun
whisper of new lives lived at sea

Your summer body taunts the gods
through your breath I drink the sky
love the winter moon
and kiss the tallest tree

-- Martha Landman

The Quickening of Seasons by Mark Lewis

21ˢᵗ January, year 1 of recognized season acceleration

Winter's end and Joe's car rattled down the road, patches of rust had settled in, the tires were worn and just about legal after a bitter, if brief, patch of snow and ice. Gentle rays of sun heralded Spring, and Joe was glad to be here, to give Simone a lift. Her company lightened his business-worn heart, even as he knew their relationship would only be of comradely utility, he was the shop manager, she was counter staff.

They talked, as they drove away, hopes for the new season.

"The scientists call it catastrophic climate change", said Joe, glancing over with a smile, "I call it a fantastic opportunity to increase our shareholder value."

"And our bonuses?"

"You bet. With the short hard winter we've already cleared out all the coats and boots and we're already gearing up for bikinis and flip flops. The weathermen say it'll be a scorcher this year, and if the summer's hot and dry as the winter was cold and icy, they'll be right."

"I heard we're due for another winter in August. Colder and shorter than the last one."

"That's the beauty of it. More extreme weather, people have to keep updating their wardrobes to stay comfy. You know what I say?"

"No but I feel sure you're going to tell me."

"Ker-ching!" He said with a cheesy wink.

He didn't notice Simone roll her eyes.

21st June, year 1 of recognized season acceleration

Summer had come and gone, burnt autumn leaves scattered along the street where Joe's new car glided in to pick up Simone. It was a convertible, but the weather was too cold and wet already to have the top down. Still, Joe had enjoyed the summer months in the new car, fruit of the high bonuses from the unprecedented profits from Spring and Summer stock.

Joe talked as they drove away, returning to his favorite subject of retail theory.

"The bikinis and summer dresses went fastest and they were sold at a premium."

"How does that work, they're made of less material aren't they?"

"We put the prices up. The less material, the skimpier, the more expensive."

"That sounds like a rip off though."

"Ah, Simone, that's why I'm management and you're staff," a toothsome grin from Joe, a hidden scowl from Simone as she looked out of the window. "Less is more. Sex sells."

"Clichés."

"A design for life, hon."

21st January, year 5 of recognized season acceleration

Autumn's end and it would be Winter again at some point tomorrow. Joe's car limped along the road, the constant and wild changes in season had been hard . Joe wiped a dribble of water away from his face where the roof leaked. If only he could afford to fix it. Simone waited for him, hood up, hard faced.

"Last day," he said.

"Kind of a sore point." she replied, getting in, leaving her hood up. "All your big plans for the store. Nowhere plans for nobody, now."

"I never thought it would come to this, I may be a retail genius but I can't control the weather or the economy" Joe said with a sigh. "Daily season changes, in-store riots. No stock rotations or new fashions for two years because the seasons change so quickly no-one can keep up. Riots in the shopping mall because food and energy bills mean no-one can afford anything."

"Retail just can't keep up with the moods Mother Earth."

"Moods? She's gone incontinent if the floods are anything to go by. If I hadn't been made redundant I'd be part exchanging this car for a boat."

"What are we going to do, Joe."

"Glad you asked. There's one growth area that I'm looking to get into, and I'll take you with me."

"Oh yes? Tell me, flood control? Rescue?"

"Oh no, too dangerous. Complaints against energy companies and their declining service and surging charges are up 500%. Bonuses for rejected complaints are rising. I've got an interview as office manager. If I get it, you'll be first in line for a call centre job, what do you think?" That grin again.

"Sounds soul destroying Joe, but just tell me. The office has guaranteed heating and lighting?"

"One of the few buildings in this city that does."

"Then count me in."

-- Mark Lewis

Heron on Ice

Pale salmon light,
9 degrees. Floor
tiles icy. Past
branches the
beaver's gnawed

at the small hole
the heron waits,
deep in the water.
Sky goes apricot,
tangerine, rose.

Suddenly, a dive,
then the heron
with sun squirming
in his mouth, a
carp that looks a

third as big as he
is gulped, then
swallowed, orange
glittering wildly
like a flag or the

wave of someone
drowning

-- Lyn Lifshin

Geese on Ice

frozen, perched as
if listening for some
distant code,
news of a warm

front coming in
time. Meanwhile,
alerts go out on
local stations,

schools close
early. The "partly
sunny" never came.
30 percent chance

of snow. Trees tilt
east, the ground
hardens. Geese
take root as scarves

float in wind like
strange new flags

-- Lyn Lifshin

Before Any Snow

you can taste it.
Before trees
glitter, a heavy
dampness after
Indian Summer.
Air's a wet
blanket. Two
sweat shirt's
aren't enough.
The gulls seem
oblivious, flap up
from across the
pond where I shiver
thru soggy grass,
descend, fifty
parachutes of feathers
skidding on pewter
glass

-- Lyn Lifshin

Trying to Just Smell the Tangerine Tree's Blossoms

the light going,
muskrats slither
toward damp stones

gold ripples
under the pond's
pewter days from

the day of the
shortest light.
Small animals

under tawny dead
reeds and lilies

as black closes in

-- *Lyn Lifshin*

Walking Past the Pond at Night

December,
record
breaking
warm. Geese
in clumps,
opalescent
under this
copper moon.
Mist, a
blue heron.
darkness wraps
my hair like
a scar
of stars

-- *Lyn Lifshin*

Chronophobic Triptych

Left Panel

The old man attends
the funeral, the words
of the priest as comfort
for those still confined,
who wait on their release
with longing and anxiety . . .

Centerpiece

He walks early spring streets
as the yellow buses stop.
He recalls when his children
filled the sidewalk and lawns
with noise and smiles and,
later, first held hands.

One August afternoon,
newlyweds move in
where the Widow Johnson
lived in a self-made nunnery.
The kids on the block feared
getting their ball from her yard.

His daughter and grandson visit
a bit more often, to keep at bay
the leaves refilling his lawn like
scarves cascading from the hat
of a stage magician called upon
to fill idle family afternoons.

This many steps to the door,
this many more to make it
down the snow-touched driveway.
Right at the corner, right, left –

no, dammit, right – and right.
Home. Fooled you again, Time.

Right Panel

Six men good and strong
to carry the slight weight,
the soulless shell alone left.
Memories grow heavier,
but in the end we leave them
to burden other shoulders.

-- Lennart Lundh

Sometimes Love is Copious

and easy-
riding like an inner-
tube down the Brazos
cold drink in one hand
sun-glasses water-
splotched lazy sun
behind scattered clouds
fingers of your empty hand
tracing a casual calligraphy
in the easy water

-- Hillary Lyon

Milagrosa

a hike in the summer heat
dusty boots and dented water bottle
a sandwich and sunblock

plumb canyons deep
with undulating trails
along the scruffy ridgeline's

rollercoaster way
steep and precipitous
an unmarked path

diverges and beckons the dirt
is smooth and shepherds
your curiosity

through the dry brush a cairn
carefully constructed
hosts a sun-lazy lizard

here your eye wanders beyond and below
to the sweeping Sonoran vista:
milagrosa

-- *Hillary Lyon*

Magnetic Bee

what pulls you up
                     pulls you over
         to the flower-flesh
in spring & everything   is sex & scent & sap

             sweet
        sickness
    like a
rising

in the blood of us all

how lovely to be small
                        yet full of sting
to be happy fat & drunk on flight
    to lap the glassy anodyne
                    drops
                     of light
to   let   go   of   every   thought   that   slakes
that   breaks
           this pull

                  -- Hillary Lyon

August Journal: Tuesday, August 6, 2013

They arrive overnight from wood stands,
backyards and gardens. Stretched across the
distant street-end, their accord is one
voice. Above the tree line along the
high-strung wires of the single file
of voltage raging towers that stride
beside the tracks—as the molten sun
rolls up—rows of countless gleaming black
starlings rise and fall back to the wires.
They are getting acquainted. The year's
young meet their elders. They tell of hawks
and how to confuse them. They discuss
the best breakfast spots. They plan for joint
flocking swirls and massive skyfalls.

-- Don Mager

Snapshot Summer

The stars unhinge themselves
A thousand candelabras,
Celestial explosion across
City swimming pools
And the love-struck
Irises of June,
Girls in their upturned toes,
The time of year when
Trees become me,
Quick as a cipher
In my jeans and books.
Manifesto of fiction,
I climb behind the eyes
Of Ginsberg and Poe,
A grinning has-been
Of the hall closet
Where I sew my girlhood
Into the frilly shelf,
A place of purity
Where baby dreams once slept,
Back before the sins
Of summer dipped
My dainty hands into
What it was to be
A woman well-read,
A woman that could stand
Before a crowd of thirty,
Unashamed the make-believe
Breast exam, the twenty minute speech,
Psychosis and cancer,
Nor the night before,
Books on the floor,
So many strange grasps
From a strange girl,
Her touch a perfect defection
Of my then-Christian fingers,

Her boyish curls
For treading fingers,
A perfect way to drown.

-- Stacy Lynn Mar

Blue Moons in Spring

I want to hang my dreams
Behind the blue moon of Spring,
Omnipresent sky God
Of Juniper and Poinsettia
Where the fedora tips of cowboy hats
Bend themselves for southern belles
Fresh in red plaid,
Their suede shoes sliding into
A thatch of clover, back garden
Becoming a sound-stage of color,
The red tips of roses tickling
Fingertips like a mischievous romantic,
Pulling noses stiff from winter
Into the atmosphere like
Old dogs resurrected for a time,
Spirits light as air and hands
Clasped for campfires where
My grandmother remembers
What it was to dance
In crowded pool rooms and
Musty banjo halls with men
She only half loved, never yet to
Worry of gray whiskers
Or the death they surely toll,
One ear singing the youngest to sleep
To a chorus of crickets and coon dogs,
And the other cajoling the days end
With the lonesome strings of Hank or Merle,
How they blew their words into her ears
On the wings of an Appalachian mountain wind.

-- Stacy Lynn Mar

Dreams of the Fisherman's House

Summer dreams are fluid,
Willowy clouds I wish upon
When the porch of my Appalachia
Is mosquito-clouded and rained out.
I long for the scent of ocean water,
Sandy terrain of beach and dunes
That lean toward the open arms of the sea,
Palm trees breaking the seal
Of an unsaid invitation.
I'd trade these itchy fields
Of dandelion and honeysuckle
For the paved maze of a sea-side village,
Perhaps the long strip of Gulf Shores
Or the shaded rocks of Half Moon Bay,
An early-morning walk against
The birdcall of seagulls and pelicans,
Jovial smile of the seamen,
Sturdy in their tanned shoulders
And straw hats as they propel
Huge nets and fishing reels
Into the dark blue, open deep.
I'd waste countless days
With my feet buried in the sand,
Eye on the wave, book on my knees,
Cabana-style umbrella waving
Against the burn of a broad sun.
I'd chase my stiff drinks with diet coke,
Straight for 32 into middle-age.
Dine at the finest restaurants,
Home-fried fish, live music,
Someone romantic to share my table,
Dark eyed in a private corner.
I'd launch my heart into
The mortared water of some

Swanky fisherman's village
And anchor away.

-- Stacy Lynn Mar

Autumn Night

Brown-ashed leaves
Crumble like forgotten webs
Of summer's hungry spiders.
I walk along a one-way street
And wonder when the moon will rise,
A roaming spotlight across this lonely night.

Scarecrow hands in a field nearby
Twitch of un-spit rain,
The sky spins a blue-pink mesh,
Lonely for a lover, perhaps Neptune.
And as I look across day-fall,
the stack of hay bales on a hill in the distance
Become an Egyptian splinx,
a gold-mouthed cat that smiles his secrets.

I am as lonely as these trees,
The thick wood nearby shivering without
The lush of leaves and seed.
Where are you, the shrill spell of night birds
That whiz the bitter truth across
Closed windows of sleeping houses
Like a black Nebuli, southbound?

The quiet is a hard, dull pull
That attracts me to empty things,
Things without beating hearts or hands for warmth…
ramshackled barns in their rusty wheels,
Church ruins without proper hymns or Gods,
And the abandoned grocery store near I75,
It's bricks as hollow as a thousand broken hearts.

-- *Stacy Lynn Mar*

Climate Change You Can Believe In

People of this great nation I address you tonight as your Prime Minister but also as a father, part of a hard working family, just like you. I know that many of you have suffered and are still suffering as I speak... Together we have been looking down the barrel of the Gulf Stream. Yes... For month after month now many parts of this great nation have suffered an influx, they have been submerged... flooded... maybe never to reappear... Those of you affected, you have my sympathies, hard-working families suffering from this influx... you have my sympathies, you *really* do. As I speak my ministers assure me that dedicated teams of experts are working round the clock to shelter you, feed you and find you new homes... but operation Soggy Yokel can only get us so far... Drastic times call for drastic measures... It's time to be honest with you. It's time that we *as a nation*, a great nation, face up to the unfaceuptoable. Our great nation, perched as it is atop a limestone plateau on the fringes of the continent has suffered, it has suffered enough, caught between the Icelandic and Azores highs it has absorbed more than its fair share of precipitation... It has suffered enough. Hard working people of this great nation it's time to say enough is enough...! Britain is full...! No more...! It is time that we as a hard-working nation of families left Europe. Yes. It is time that Britain left Europe... and headed for the Caribbean! Yes. As I speak my ministers assure me that dedicated teams of experts are working on detaching the British Isles from the ocean floor and when they achieve this the entire British fleet will be engaged to tug this great nation out into the mid-Atlantic... and beyond. People of this great nation you gave me a slim majority at the last election, and I thank you for that. Now I pledge by the end of this parliament Britain will be a tropical country, and *that* is climate change you can believe in!

-- Adam Marks

Seasons

Winter: You buy a plant at Whole Foods, something like a small fir tree, and place it on a table. Her best friend sends you a glass chick ornament and you hang it on your plant. Boxes of decorations sit untouched in the cellar. Friends invite you to dinner, and you go, wearing her sweater, her pearls. You wear them every day. There's a new year about to happen, you hear. After Christmas comes New Year's. Maybe you'll travel somewhere; it doesn't matter where you go. Her message is still on your phone machine: "Mom! Call me. I have some good news!"

Fall: A call comes in to tell you she has died. She died suddenly in her sleep. Your phone is in the kitchen; you sit there holding it. Your kitchen is yellow and orange and turquoise and you sit there, still clutching a dishtowel. The towel is embroidered with chicks. You fly to her apartment, your ticket for the following week reassigned to this one. Her apartment is a stage set, the postcard you mailed last week on her coffee table. You arrange a funeral and can't think who this is all for, even when you look at her in the coffin. You fly back home where people are still living lives. You get word that her project was a huge success. Her gold-embossed certificate is forwarded to you.

Summer: She arrives at the airport, all smiles, at last at last. There's time to see a play, to hike Point Reyes. You lunch at a café. I got the project in, she says. Happy Fourth of July, you say, watching the sprays of blue and explosions of red and white in the sky over Dolores Park. Peter has broken up with me, she says. I think I'll be all right though, she said. We'll go shopping, you say. I'm just so tired, she says. Well, you can rest up now, you say, taking pictures at the Zoo, even on the sidewalk in front of the airport terminal, not wanting to give her up.

Spring: You thought maybe you'd visit her, maybe you'd fly out. She says, Don't bother, Mom, I'll see you this summer. I'm just thrilled my project got the go-ahead. I have too much work to do and we won't have enough time together. It'll be more fun later. It's true: your schedules are out of sync and there's summer, and fall, and Christmas.

Okay, then. You send her a grass green leather wallet. She sends you a card, a scarf with daffodils. Your gifts include chicks—fuzzy ones and marshmallow ones—a joke, a custom, between you. Happy Easter, you say, Happy Spring.

-- Jackie Davis Martin

Stone with Memory

The statue of the woman stood stone still in the park. Her carefully carved youth endured the glaring sun and the blistering cold wind and outlasted the benches and the trees and every child who came to play there. Most people said she was beautiful, but they were blind to her one desire, to see the beauty they all said she had. The water pouring from the vase in her hands and the angle of her head made it impossible.

Instead of herself, she saw petals drift down from the branch above and settle in the water around her feet. A woman sitting on a nearby bench sneezed. A man sat down beside her, calling her "Gianna" in a tainted tone, trying to stroke a piece of her long hair. Their tones rose to an urgent, unpleasant crescendo before Gianna yelled and stormed off, leaving the man to a sudden deluge without an umbrella.

As he walked away, the statue watched as something dangerous took root in him.

Eventually, the snow of petals disappeared, replaced by the nearly continual call of, "Ice cream, ice cream!" issuing from the old man wheeling a food cart. At the end of every day, the vendor sat on the edge of the statue's fountain and ate his remaining product with whatever company felt like joining him. Many times, it was a boy with holes in his shirt and bare feet. Once or twice, it was Gianna, who salted her vanilla cone with tears. The man accepted no money for these things; their words were payment enough before he went home to his inevitably empty apartment, the same way many had before him.

One sweltering night among the distant call of traffic, the man came back and told the statue that he was going to take Gianna away whether she liked it or not. The dangerous thing had bloomed. That knowledge and his words ossified into memories long before his silhouette disappeared from her sight.

The leaves turned to fire and melted the call of "Ice cream, ice cream!" When the park grew quieter, she began trying to see herself, and even though she looked, the water—her only mirror—ripped constantly. She knew of the beauty and ugliness in people, formed by countless sedimentary memories, yet she wondered what standards human beings based their shorter-lived opinions on. Behind her attempts followed a blaze of yearning for the motion most people were lucky to possess. Then, she could look. Then, she could do something about the man with the ugly voice.

That yearning cooled and crystallized once the world grew white and walled the statue off from the world that called her beautiful. She spent the cold days remembering the man with the dangerous blossom inside of him and wondering if it had withered or if it still stuck in him like a thorn. Although she tried once again to see the beauty people often told her she had, the ice around her feet was clouded and reflected nothing but the drastic change in weather.

The man came back in darkness, crossing the sidewalk with his hands in his pockets. As he approached, her desire for motion blazed to life, but her feet remained stubbornly stone, and the snow and ice remained as frozen as she was. He stepped onto the lip of her fountain, sweeping her white walls away, cradling an object in his hand. He struck repeated, laborious blows, but she couldn't properly feel the pain through her shock, not even as she fell to pieces. A police woman shouted and pursued the vandal. The statue couldn't recall, but the voice and the face reminded her of someone she had seen before.

What was left of the statue entered an infirmary of ice and snow and slow, reluctant forgetting. Eventually, green buds dotted the branches above her head, and the world forgave itself for being cruel. "I caught him in the end," a woman told the statue, armless but otherwise unharmed. "I'm just sorry I didn't get here before it was too late." The woman spoke as if she had known the statue, as if some mysterious "him" had broken her arms off. The statue's expression never thawed, not even when the city planners carried her away to be forgotten. As they carried her broken form over the water, she finally had a chance to see her own beauty.

If only she had remembered to look.

-- Amanda M. May

Anopheles

Lying over a towel,
a bikinied woman
enjoyed feeling her body
drink up the temperature.

The woman's every pore
wished the day
were a downloadable video,
replaying at her will.

Unbeknownst to the woman,
a man,
owning another view,
hated the temperature.
No temperature could terminate
his mental hurricane.

Years ago,
one woodland mosquito
withdrew his wife's warmth
and deposited malaria's fever.

Glaring at the large shoreline
made him remember
when he told his wife
this beach was their writing pad,
a writing pad awaiting the statement,
"I love you."

Since her death,
the beach
could not hold
all the terms defining his pain.

-- *Bob McNeil*

Beach

My mind is an ocean
where swimmers, surfers,
sun worshippers cavort.

Long salty hair
held between
their teeth.
Flourishing
wild flowered gowns
                    . . . streams of silk
                        waves of taffeta
                            splashy lace.

They sail through
my watery face
combing my eyes
whispering in my ears.

Alone, under a pointillist sky.
Gulls flying around me.
Black waters touched by
moon of vague prophecy.

-- *Joan McNerney*

Sold

This morning's setting moon appears
   a gibbous ghost snared by cloud wraiths,
      what remains of February's wet rage.

Like a widow, her glow fading, unable
   to cast shadows, she sheds
      only shallow beams through

tortuous limbs of a dying live oak.
   Or like a tropical banshee silenced
      in draperies of Spanish moss,

dry robes tattered to strands,
   this waning shine fails to keen.
      She fancies the bristling fur

of thick resurrection fern,
   the shagged manes of winter's
      emaciated panthers. In descent,

as if fallen to her knees on Earth's
   grim horizon, she mourns
      night's spoils with day's earliest

vultures rustling their appetite for carrion.
   Our moon's lamentation, her primal
      whimpering, is the death-clatter voice

of sable palm fronds. Soon the moon,
   more and more muted, will say nothing
      of the truth she knows

about the skeletons in Florida's
   coffin. One last remnant of dim light
     is so like property condemned.

-- Karla Linn Merrifield

Summer Love

Short somnolent night
hangs precariously by a fragile thread
that may snap any time
and be blown away by a diffident Loo
or be swept away by the torrential breaths
through the ravines and slopes
riding the ripples of sweat and sighs
towards the eventual estuary
where the saline tongue of the sea
will lap it up and suck it to oblivion.

This night tasting an indifferent summer
will be lost in the Milky Way leading to
an infinite galaxy of stars
and evaporate under the eye lashes
of a sweltering dawn
while the panting of tired torsos slowly
will attenuate to a decadent rhythm
the silver oak trees will stand still
their outlines becoming sharper and sharper.
and a rooster will crow and give the wake up call.

-- Dilip Mohapatra

Of Firewood and Winter Sky

Winter is the time for fire. Wood in the
loaded wheelbarrow becomes clumps of
old books, concentric rings holy texts only
a nature monk can read.
Split sticks, encapsulated fusion of light
from the sky. Moved here by hands
that trace the sun's sacrament, knowing
when the tree was felled in summer,
communion of wood and fire would be
consummated by winter's cremation.
Reduced to snowy ash, flames as multiple
kaleidoscope iguana tongues flicking
behind the stove's glass—trinity formed between
flesh and wood, fire—Balanos, hamadryad,
that beckoned when saw bit trunk, honored
totem, your sacrifice, creation of light where
only the suppliant sees traced against the sky.

-- *Ralph Monday*

September

A Vivaldi odyssey, metronomic movement
like a hemlock tuning fork arranging seasonal
harmonics for the annual ache—a frosty tooth,
long neglected kissing the virgin while contemplating
the justice yet to be weighed.

      Nine labors passed—throated singers
         Melancholic buried within their own
            Time capsule awaiting the sleeping ram.

The muted youth will come in nitroglycerine waves
like photons scattered willy nilly by a solar flare
galloping photosultry phantoms eager to put
some different English on the spin

      Where rocky hues
         Complement shedding trees
         Like a fragile old woman

Combing her hair in the last, long sweet fragility--
a dreaming life reverie envisioned in the chalky
faces of lovers' shades—a conclusive tempting taste
of monthly smorgasbord lying delicate and bitter
on the palate

      Teasing the fragile primate tissue
         Processing hinted images of
            Hardy inclinations already forgotten

Done away by the meandering slow strokes
of comedic masked seasons playing out
an eternal pantomime like a last rattled thump
settling in for the show.

            -- Ralph Monday

The Winter Solstice, a Sun is Born

The sun mutes conversation on this day,
Lacking energy, a rundown clock needing
New springs it broods over Christmas parties,
Lacks salvation for saturnalia amid modern
Tinkle of cocktail glass, drunken laughter,
All the strung lights that flicker, cinema
Points run frame by ancient frame, illustrating
The unconscious need for light the way that
A brutish cave dweller would have seen his
Soul in red embers cathedraling his dark door
Where he offered the magic of fire to a great
Ball of western light—naples yellow, autumn
Russet barely etching the frightened horizon,
Fading away like smoke sucked by a vacuum—
Or the pulsebeat Stonehenge drums presided
Over by a priestess with snake eyes that sees
The gods beginning return, flame wisp through
Crack in stone.
The ones in jean and shirt, skirt and blouse
That cannot tongue-talk the unseen, cannot
Fear-dance the light's demise for their mother,
Father, is machine, blood earned oil, electricity
Gathering them up so that they crackle, hiss
Sputter like meat above raked coals. The cities they
walk through, babel towers, sprouted upward, windows
blind glass eyes, stubs without a seer.
This is the soft god, voiceless prophet trapping
Them within bounded walls. When they lie
Naked in bed, bodies united like mortared bricks,
They do not understand why the sun is born,
cannot cipher what they fear.

-- Ralph Monday

The Hearer

An awareness of twilight is regarded
in the rime caked limbs, bare trees bent against
the sleet assaulting like stone a lengthy spell.
To witness the woody skeletons bent and jagged
in the cold glimmer of the March moon, to
consider the blank desolation in
black forms, misery a crust of needles,
the cry of caves raging at a living
storm, is to be a hearer—something only
who heeds in the ice, watches a dire moment.
Knowing that the time of being is but
the same noise of rare needles girdled away,
passing through the forest of thought until
moment's ticking impression, no more than a reverie.

-- Ralph Monday

Moontime in the Blood

The grandmother told her twelve year old
granddaughter *you can't go in the garden.*
Why grandma?
Because you are bleeding and it will ruin the
plants. I killed a whole bed of cucumbers once.
I paused from hoeing tomatoes and pondered the
significance of this conversation passed from aged
female to young girl.
The myth of blood. Should we build a grass hut
and banish her to the moonlodge for a week? Should we
make a menses mound and call on lost Eve to come and
remove the curse?
Once upon a time the ancient Hindus believed that
all life is created from the thickened blood of the
great mother.
Once upon a time the moon moved through the
skies and moved the blood of the woman, the tides,
like some medieval angel tethered to the planets, and
the blood of the people moved with the thick flow.
Once upon a time the bleeding day did not wilt plants,
dry seeds, or cause fruit to fall spotted and rotten.
Once upon a time…but not today…as the
grandmother hurried her away.

-- *Ralph Monday*

Late February Snow

Beginning with a line by Joseph Stroud*

See how the snow drifts down, look how happy
the children are as they throw themselves on the ground,
wave their wings, angelic giggles spilling from their lips.
Watch as they gather great balls of snow, sculpt it
into a carrot-nosed man, a cat resting on its side,
a roaring lion decorated with a dog collar and blue
plastic-lid eyes. Look how carefree they are, arms
outstretched, examining each individual snow crystal
landing on dark sleeves. Watch sleds pick up speed
as they zip down the hill, skates cutting figures
on the moonlit lake, youngsters climbing heaps
of snow at the end of the cul de sac, squealing
as they slide to the ground on the seats of their pants.

The white flakes drift down and down till grown ups
like me say, *No more. I can't wait till spring.*
But I'm grateful to the children happily playing
in piles of snow before it melts, reminding me
how blissful snow made me before I learned
to drive, before I feared a fall, before the child
in me was covered with the blanket of adulthood,
buried like crocuses beneath the snow.

-- Wilda Morris

**The first line is from "Manna," Of This World and Selected
Poems (Copper Canyon Press, 1998).*

In the January Chill

Trees, weighed down
by parkas of snow,
line the road.
Silence owns the woods
on this cold January night.

The lake wears a poncho of ice.
My fingers tingle in too-thin gloves.
My boots no longer
keep out the cold.

There has always been warmth
awaiting my return,
Dad wanting to carry my suitcase,
Mother offering hot chocolate.

I trace the path back
to an empty home.

-- Wilda Morris

Claire and the Wind

My two year old granddaughter is fairy like, with blond hair that curls at the ends. From her very first day outside, whenever a breeze grazed her hazel eyes, she would close them and a smile would come to her two little lips. I live on the top of a hill near the ocean and in the spring the breeze is especially soft with the floating scents of star jasmine and lavender. Claire closes her eyes while her nostrils move in and out. She stands very still.

"Hmmm," she says, then she looks at me wide-eyed. What is in that tiny brain as the gusts travel through her pale locks?

She only giggles when I say, "Claire likes the wind."

I bought her a small plastic pinwheel with a ladybug in the middle, thinking she could blow on it when the air was still. She could make her own wind. She stuck it into a flowerless flower pot facing the ocean and it began to move in colorful circles.

"Hmmm," she murmurs.

Summers are filled with days when we wake to fog and watch as it slowly drifts away until at about noon it is sunny and bright. Claire and I march down to my old arena and play in the sand or pull the endless weeds, the cats following us to perch themselves on the chairs. The moving fog brings its own wet wind. Everything gets a little damp, even the cats. Claire's ringlets stick to her face. In between shovels of sand, her chubby little hands make the mist curl and wave.

"Look," I tell her. "Claire is making the wind fog move."

"Hmmm," she says and then dumps a scoop of sand on a reclining cat that never moves because he is getting her attention.

Fall is hot and sometimes we saunter down to the barn to wait for the ocean to send some cooling air. Claire will stand at the edge of the

breezeway looking way out to sea. "The ocean breeze is coming," I tell her. She sits quietly on a step stool petting one cat then the other. Finally a burst of air will travel in through the rafters making a swooshing sound.

"Hmmm," she says.

Winter can be chilly and soggy, but Claire will hit the glass of the sliding door, insisting to go out, so we pass through the garage by the cats huddled next to each other, meowing. They know better. Outside the air currents can be quite strong, cold and persistent. She has a pink knitted cap I keep for her that she puts on by herself. At first sometimes she just stands next to the house, letting the wind whip around her face and closing her eyes yet moving her hands as if she might take off like a butterfly. I would love to know what this wind fascination is but she isn't able to make those kinds of explanations yet, so we make our bundled way down to the gate for the mail. The wind might whip roughly around but leftover rain puddles are calling to Claire. She jumps in every one. Her hat flies off and she giggles but happily stands still as a momentary strong breeze whisks her face.

"Hmmm," she says.

My husband bought a large copper wind sculpture and positioned it in the ground between the barn and the house. "I think Claire will like this," he said as he stood back to watch it begin to move with the afternoon wind. Its burnished leaves glide in circles, spiraling round and round.

"Hmmm," I said smiling.

-- *Carol Murphy*

Black Ice

Sleet obscured my view; bent me
Toward the wipers' drone.

None ahead or behind.

My bright world right
To link will to a well-known machine
Asserted.

But I swerved – breath held – the tires bit,
Yanked me back.

White lines, asphalt
Reappeared; I could hear
The radio again.

-- Joseph Murphy

Four Seasons Haiku

after heaven's cymbals
a concerto of hard rain
a solo bud

the troupe is ready—
it is time to find a patch
of perfect lawn grass

who let in the wind?
it has blown a dying leaf
on to my pillow

there is only snow
like the memory of doves—
shavings and feathers

-- Lee Nash

Tongue Speak

The tip of my tongue
holds your attention.

You slip into my rosewater
kindness recalling
the golden dust of lilies
from an earlier time.

I smash into your slash of overgrown words
expecting my serpentine doubts
to skip, chiseled pebbles
sliding over silvery sea.

you have come home

but I can't find you anywhere.
Not In the envelope of this muddy silence

where I wait with my hand beaten grief.

You clasp a different package
against your ruined chest
as though the wrapping can keep you safe.

Now it's summer mornings
that smear my sibilant sorrow
with the quiet hum of lilacs and grasses
held in small relief.

You hide in the stomach of a lion
the distance between us

is only a swallow

a slip of rings and promises neither of us
can keep.

Heat pushes past deliberation

of the cost of 98 cent tomatoes

or the weight of this useless love.

The air is still redolent
of a remembered touch

when our oxygen levels never climbed

over zero. You whirled
a thigh sliding tango with me
and I fell like a shot bird
into your troubling arms.

Soon we'll both disappear, bubbles

leaving no footprints

across this tundra landscape
of the veil.

-- Jude Neale

Spring Dead

There's a dead man in the attic.

I don't want to cope with that now.
First I'll eat an apple, maybe write a poem.
Later, this afternoon, I'll deal. Not now.
The sun is shining, it's spring, and life is starting fresh.
The seed of the apple I just ate is green inside its husk,
a new tree eager to grow.

Even though Jo stripped branches from the little weeping
cherry
that would have bloomed a huge bouquet,
sap still runs up that stem,
and next year it will show its glory.
Everywhere I look, bulbs peek out,
ferns unfurl.

Who needs death today?

-- Mary Newell

Morning of All Mornings

The morning is shrouded in cigarette smoke,
And stuffed full of pastries and olives.
The woman she is can't manage a minute,
Of coffee and croissants and casual chat,
without missing the point entirely.
She sips from a cup and she sucks on a smoke
And she questions his every remark.

With each of his words are spat ten more of hers,
To harass it and trip it face first in the ashtray.
So he ceases to speak and she sits in a sulk,
All sullen and listless as the mountains around her;
Eyes stirring coffee that's barely a mouthful,
But somehow a lifetime.
With an eyebrow the refill,
But she remains utterly unfulfilled.
Cool as a thing and the morning itself,
But the blue of her eyes is amelt with the red of her mood.
The feeling's exclusive,
But still she rolls looks to his side of a one-sided fight.

His vignettes are splattered with vinaigrette,
Turning words into purpley petals,
While the spinach itself digests.
Napkins that dabble in diet and closure_
Are stacked up in sixes between them.
But her humorlessness will accumulate
In a battering ram of lugubriousness.
That's eyebrows raised beyond the usual rate;
Not gentle pistes but a furry cliff from which her hair line peers.

Salad days are seasoned by his older age;
A novel in the works will only work the rift between them
Further from the golden age.
But that's ok, he thinks,
Her aggravation only aggravates his funny bone.

Her quibbles linger vaguely on his brain,
But all the rest just washes through his guts
Like weak and fruitless tea.

Cigarette in hand,
The smoke to mingle with the morning mist,
The chalets mingle with the street lamps
And trickle down the streets.
The frost has tiptoed up the hillside
Whilst a damp and vernal precedent takes hold.

A ping-pong match of rolling eyes takes place across the table.
What started as a playful rally,
Ricochets into the hateful.
Serving words to pickle faces beetroot red embarrassed,
Middle fingers swat her glares
As croissant crumbs propel across the table.
Chitchat lunges from the trifling
To a turbine through the skull.
Lightning strikes a cloudless morning.
City squares dismantled brick by brick throughout the rising heat.

The ashtray craves the ashes,
Shrugged so easily into its mouth.
Her savage words serve only as temptation,
For the entrails of their marriage
Dangle centimeters from destruction.
It slobbers as the blood and guts of married life
Are tossed around the café.
Accusations sloshed unsparingly,
She scoffs in blood-red apathy.
A man so wishy-washy in his words
Has washed up writing self-help journals.
The hilarity. Calamity.
Catastrophe in miniature.

Another coffee, as the weather cools.
The leaves have fallen with the realization

That this marriage has its seasons.
And this may not be one.

-- Reeve Nicholls

Wild Roses

Entangled by focused words
and a metaphor
in a divine parachute
and wounded umbrellas
in the Spanish speaking rain
among sister's wild roses
you wave by the seas
nodding to adolescence
among the presence
of grinning sunflowers
foraging for a glimpse
of bread on a summer day
fleeing the greenhouses
you dream and tremble
for simple things
like neon butterflies
in the mountains
escaping troubles,
no memory holds you back
among a songbird woodland.

-- BZ Niditch

Constable's Landscapes

Invincible paint
of sky blue haze
with patches of hilly light
splashed on my eyes
still dripping
in my admiring gesture
with birds
at close distance
with questions,
but who can answer
from my camera's flash light
from the heights of trees
by cosmic intuition
of unexplored waterfalls
by the ocean air
escaping my riffs
in a woodwind of fragility
testing my own shapeless
knowledge of words
in pictures of being alive.

-- BZ Niditch

Freesia in Winter

Trouble can't find me here.
Stars, the dogs of ice,
shine down on the smooth
blackness of my earthen bed.
Muffled by dirt, I hold my breath,
waiting for a change.

Shivering in my brown fur overcoat,
and my sprouted night cap,
I wait like a mole.
I have no vision.
Is anyone there?

Tendrils of root reach out
like a blind man reaches out
with his white cane.

The rain falls like big shoes
walking overhead.
I am a cemetery.
I survive on earthworms,
bits of shell and remembered songs.

I wait for change.
Was that warmth?
Was that light?
Was that birdsong?

At last I push aside
my coverlet of leaves
and stretch my stems,
stretching them to the sun.
Soon there will be a celebration,
a homecoming.

In appreciation,
I will bring fragrant white
blossoms to share.

-- *Suzanne O'Connell*

The Crab Apple Tree

the blades of the crab-apple tree
whisper to me
and tear the hair of jagged crows

black branches tie themselves in knots

the leaves are yellow this year
and there are no cedar waxwings

soon the crab-apple tree will sing
the song of its bitter
fruit
and
the pale summer sun will stand still
      and
       listen.

-- Norman J. Olson

Spring: Is Anybody Listening to the Trees?

every tree trunk
is screaming in pain
like a
junkie
looking for love and
reconciliation
in
a needle

the fat is in the fire for sure this time

my fingers are ice cubes
and my eyes
are pits of acid…

why would you care what I have to say?

-- Norman J. Olson

Shadow Lake Snow Snakes

not the inviting cotton candy snow
scene on a holiday greeting card
or sparkling fluffy flakes floating
softly in the shaken crystal globe

these wind whipped ice shards blown
thrown stinging not sticking hurled
swirled across bare brown ground like
long white snakes slithering in the sand

-- Carl Palmer

Engaging Vancouver, B.C.

Along the beach near Jericho Park
a family and a loner strolled
exchanging with the sun warmth
to gather calm - weathering

autumn in their face and summer
in their arms. In oscillating visions
before the mountains, exploring
tracks and trails, May moved on

to sketch a sled, skis, a sleigh,
asking other days to note that
October leaves to dwell with
November and December,

hailing years of engagement,
observation and endeavor,
along the slopes of possibly forever, venture's bracing clay.

-- Joyce Parkes

You wash this floor the way winter
waits for its ice to stir
show more interest in coming closer

and the drowned —what bubbles up
is bottom sand though you drift
and further out more water

unable to dry so far from home
--a single drop by drop
wipes down the world and longing

--it's how you sleep
leaking from your pores
this side then that breaking open

holding on to each other and now
without shape, making it through
as surfaces and nearer.

-- Simon Perchik

The Plains of Venezuela

Winter has never brought us a snowflake.
Come spring, our growing lands are seared,
and these we burn as is our tradition—
dead overgrowth serves as tinder.

Cleared of desiccation by consumptive fire,
our parched fields await the rains—
balm of life for the savanna
and healer of heat-cracked soil.

Scrub cattle flick string-tails
at swarms of parasites droning.
Weakened grazers shelter near a gnarled tree
as the season's first thunderstorm begins.

As dull thuds raise small puffs of dust
it is time for the earth and ourselves to be healed.
Soon, the scarlet ibis will find the red crab
and blooms from the deluge bead the bleak horizon.

As ever, the burst of rain will cease,
and again, the father star will scorch mother earth
and again, we shall fire our fields to tender the flood—
as it has been throughout our history and also before.

I believe these cycles of death and life to be true,
for as grayness prospers and muscles wither,
I watch a scarlet ibis circle over vast plains
drifted with the heaviness of a choking winter.

-- Richard King Perkins II

Autumn in Aqua Immemorial

There was a night, perhaps, when you might have loved me—
the night we danced and kissed and plucked blazing stars
from the autumn sky for play.

As death cannot leave any of us enough alone
within every wincing thought may the malabar seed descend—
for into the flaxen earth shall sadness
bequeath our repeated motions of drowning.

Chamomile shall hearken the breaking of autumn
and the immemorial few still waiting for love's unlikely return
will release luminously from within the most shallow span of arms.

I think we were two young immortals that night,
naively toying with the substance of a vulnerable universe—
where old men return to checkers and faded playing cards
while their wives go shopping for compression socks
and organ meat only because it is autumn.

My blameworthy hands tread currents of frail white daisies
becoming a fleeting school of silver fish
in a suspension of might have been.

Fin tips will skim the leaves and feathers of your being
and love momentarily deliver life
as the scimitar-bearing grain-thief softly swishes nearby
with the sudden impact and blessing of air.

I was therefore puzzled when you returned to pulling weeds
in a malnourished garden with him,

leaving me to toil at replacing our bushels of pilfered stars
that don't seem to shine so brightly now.

In eventual autumn, the earth is aqua fading;
when the great agile grain-thief blinds intimately—

-- Richard King Perkins II

Winter Into Spring

All winter the clouds bore down on us
like stacks of mattresses we had to
carry everywhere on our heads, our
bent backs and shoulders.

Now in spring we can't find a trace
of these burdens and wonder where we
laid them, who took them and whether
there's any residue to sweep up.

Our spines slowly readjust, causing us
to walk lighter, taller, without
scraping our feet on road salt, concrete
and ice.

Is this some kind of trick? Will we be
pounded into the ground by falling futons
the moment we express relief?

Is blue sky just an illusion of youth,
lightheartedness, an absence of cares
that will open like a secret door on
a storehouse of ripened horrors?

We have seen and borne too much to
trust this lightness to last, that our
burdens won't be heaped back on us
at the close of the act.

And yet, while we can, we gaze up and
admire the beauty and brightness that
had seemed so distant — for an instant
not letting forebodings unhinge us.

-- Georgia Ressmeyer

Summer Doldrums

All day I wait
for a flicker of weather
a blink
toe-tap
strand of hair slipping
    out of a barrette
facial tic
hint of breath

Death is
wax
cement
shellac

In time I'm sure to get
a second wind
come dancing from
my grave
mood
to match a lively gust
if gusts resume

Do gusts forget?

Will I remember
every step?

-- Georgia Ressmeyer

Eyes On Fire

When sight is scorched by flaming
leaves in fall, sun's surcharge seems
punitive.

Mist becomes the preferred medium,
dousing the harshest glare of autumn's
peak-week flamboyance.

My eyes cannot endure prolonged
exposure to searing reds and yellows,
bonfires of colors torching lashes,
lids, turning retinas to embers.

After a while it's mist I crave, water
and blackness, coolness and moisture
extinguishing the pain of taking in
so much blistering beauty.

Come to me with soothing ointment,
nighttime. Ease these eye-seizures
with cooing sounds, a flurry of soft
wings.

-- Georgia Ressmeyer

England through the Seasons

Spring

The first spring blooms push through the frosty earth heralding the end of winter. A sign of hope, new life and a new beginning.

It's cold. They thought England would be warmer. The lorry pulls into the lay-by. They climb out and stretch aching limbs, treading on the snowdrops and crocuses on the grass verge. They wait in the midnight darkness, hungry and thirsty. A van pulls up. A man hands money over to the lorry driver. He shouts for them to get into his van in broken Russian. He confiscates their passports and tells them that they owe him £5,000 each for transport and accommodation. One of them protests, he already paid £8,000 at Vilnius airport. He is punched in the face. Their owner drives them to their lodgings - a dilapidated barn. He locks them in. This is not what they expected.

Today they will work for 20 hours straight.

It is flower picking season in Cornwall.

Summer

Nowhere is better in the summer than England. Everyone is happy; the days are longer; the vegetation is lush. A group of schoolgirls celebrate with a paddle in the fountain at Trafalgar Square. They have finished school for good, they are free.

She arrives at Heathrow travel-weary but excited. This is a new beginning, she will be a receptionist at an expensive hotel. Her boyfriend promises to join her to share the adventure; but he will never contact her again.

She is met by a woman who confiscates her passport. She paid £3,000 to the agency back home in Albania, but now she owes the woman £30,000. To repay the debt she must work for the woman. Her accommodation is a brothel. Her first client is waiting in the next room. She is 18 but looks 15 so she will make lots of money. This is not what she expected.

She pleads with the woman, who slaps her. Today she will work for 20 hours straight.

It is the height of the tourist season in London.

Autumn

The brambles are ripe with berries. The ground is bursting with potatoes. The last crop of tomatoes need picking with nimble hands. The weather is hazy.

The farmer does not like waste and docks wages. It is back breaking work. The girls have smaller hands so they pick the fruit, the boys work in the fields. They still haven't been paid and it's been a month. The farmer says he gives the money to their gang master, who is in charge of wages and accommodation. Their room is basic, they all sleep in one space, and there isn't electricity or running water. They have as much vodka as they want but never enough sleep. One of the boys asks why they haven't been paid. The gang master says they all owe him for their food and lodgings. They will get their wages when they have paid their debt. This is not what they expected. A girl complains that she is exhausted. He breaks her nose.

Today they will work for 20 hours straight. And they will never complain again.

It is Harvest in Lincolnshire.

Winter

The gradual excitement and expectation of Christmas is contagious. Everything is red, green and gold. Children post their letters to Lapland hoping that Santa will come. It is a time for families and friends to eat, drink and be merry.

Her family is destitute but there might be a way to escape the shame of poverty. Her Uncle is an important man in England and her Auntie needs help around the house. The flight from Vietnam was long. Auntie met her at the airport, she embraced her, how grown up she was for 12. Auntie's house was the largest she had ever seen with many rooms and big gates. She was given her daily duties: all the cleaning, laundry, the cooking, nannying the 4 children. She can only leave the house to pick up the children from school. She mustn't talk to anyone; she can't speak English anyway. Auntie tells her she is an illegal immigrant. If the police find her they will beat her with sticks. Her bed is the floor of the unheated outhouse; her meals are the scraps from the Christmas parties. This is not what she expected. She is frightened and wants her mum. But her mum never calls.

Today, tomorrow and forever she will work for 20 hours straight.

It is the season of good will in England.

-- Pippa Rowen

history is here
to tell us that phone numbers
and shoestrings used to
be shorter, days were longer,
and summer skies much bluer

-- Tom Russell

Wallpaper

The stream running across the desktop reflects
her quiet blue patience as she stands there surrounded

by shortcuts that would take her where she's never been.
The heron seems distracted by the Word

icon next to the recycle bin and will stay hungry
if she searches files and folders for fish.

She needs to launch her face into the cool April
habitat at her feet for something more substantial

than cyber fins and coded tails.
And don't wait too long my proud, pompous friend.

The darkest of nights may be only seconds away.

-- Tom Russell

Ode to the August Rose Bush

It was pink and cream and perfectly soft.
It moved and smoothed in languid waves,
like a summer sunlit satin dress,
and big-smiled so juice-dripping wide
that it made my own mouth water, how full
and ripe it was, just there, my rose
on the tip of a hot, late-August branch,
doing nothing all summer long
but learning how to dangle, so
helplessly delicate, breeze-tossed it was
a slow-bobbing lost little sailboat,
unmanned and adrift in the wild world
of men in gardens, and waiting just for me.
And so it drew me in, and then enflamed me.
I took the flower in my hands and
thumbed apart the dew-soft petals
so my nose could shove down in
there, deep to where the scent was
crooning me on with its climbing, curly-tendrilled
promises of more—that scent,
you understand, makes men do things
like take deep breaths, just to be
submerged and nestle all within the rose,
to be sound and lost entirely, in the tight, rare, secret
space of scent and nostril.

What wicked beauty,
nature gives her roses,
I thought (inhaling all)
just before September.

-- *Mary Salen*

Teeming

Cities dance.
Sharp linear shapes
slapping your face.
Assaulting you with grey grit
leaving you dazed.
Catch teeming life sights
around each corner.

Winter seals, draped with fur coats,
narrowly miss denizens with their tusks.
Foxes in well-tailored red
trot amongst crowds.
Wolves in white robes
sing gospel songs.
Umbrella toting penguins
bring little luck on wet streets.

Bullfrogs busk in spring
crooning for cash.
Tawny cicadas play the rhythm.
Snow hares change white to brown.
Zombies rise out of doorways
scare the migrating flocks.

Summer coxcombs come to catch
pecking hens and crowing roosters.
Buffalo herds shorn of winter's
hoary coat samba on the mall.
Calves slurp ice rainbows chew churros
lost to their parents in fresh dreams
Armani stallions
stage an orchestra of bop.

-- Paul Sasges

My Dead

The high blue skies of summer
hardly match your sorrow—
a sky, lowering and grey,
would better correspond.

My dead have always died
in winter. It's true!
Born in spring and summer, we curl
upon ourselves at winter's fright.

It makes sense, the rest
of the southern world dying then,
me included, a tight knot
of lament for summer's loss.

But grief knows no seasons,
no gentle pass from cold and night
to heat and light, no healing time.
Trust only Valium and Scotch

to stifle the clangor of the knife,
my face in the mirror red and botched
somehow by another mourning.
Eyes fill, tears fall,

a gargoyle mouth screams shut.
Dead and gone! I'm left
to fashion what memories I can
from dreams I carry in my blood.

-- Francesca Sasnaitis

Propane shortage
in the middle of winter
Midwestern hell

-- Emily Jo Scalzo

lightning rakes the sky
the bus shudders in the wind
first spring thunderstorm

-- Emily Jo Scalzo

Blizzard

Meteorologist are having a
field day – catastrophic storm
no an apocalypse of a storm
a disaster in the making

The politicians are on TV to
hear themselves and look good
telling everyone to take this
seriously and shop now

So the streets are all crammed
with crazed drivers while the
supermarket is filled with the insane
pushing and shoving for a cereal

Or a dozen chicken wings, meat
fruit, vegetables and whatever
someone else has not grabbed
and the first flake hasn't even landed

-- Zvi A. Sesling

Winter

bare trees reach and stretch
to greet the morning weather—
nature's yoga moves.

-- Jo Simons

Even Sins

I don't need to drink
to look drunk out here.
Between the house and barn
I walk.
Wind blows so hard
even animals
stagger.
Clouds like silverware
fork their tongues
poke at my weaknesses.
I never claim to be an angel
but I feel my wings stiffen
under my winter jacket.
Coats of snow
whiten and hide
almost everything
even sins.

-- Rosemary Marshall Staples

Grand Seasons & Grandsons

I heard the voices of geese at dusk
noticed the aspen had begun
to trade colors with the sun
hues of green for yellow-gold
a bull-throated cricket
sang its song for me
as darkness slipped its moorings
claimed me as one of its shadows

my favorite time of year
autumn
reminds me of you
son of my son
the time of your arrival
the perfect symmetry of your being

-- Tom Sterner

Promenade

she is a parade of seasons
a wandering minstrel
singing the moon
dancing the sun
day is hers to bestow
7 night divide
creatures pressed to her skin
driven a-wander
her awesome tide
uninspired by miracles
there are none to which
her heart ascribes
more to be lovely
than loved is her way
a passion of rainbows
thunder ignites
bolts of lightning
unexpected
star sprinkled visits
pinned to darkness
dimensions of gods
graffiti, her leaves
o'er a parade that ne'er ends

-- Tom Sterner

The Garden of the Tuileries on a Winter Afternoon

-- after The Garden of the Tuileries on a Winter Afternoon,
artist Camille Pissarro, 1899

Not a small park with elfin architectures,
but vast corridors where the eye defines history.
I wear frayed gabardine, my worn top-hat,
let the brief hours decide slower steps. Stratus clouds,
yellow and blue, scratch a paler sky, topaz and azure
caught in leathery trees, those mellow colors
just before a hard freeze. Shreds of summer balloons,
once happy orbs, snag in ancient elms. Gone
are carts selling feather monkeys and shiny
vessels cast by tiny hands across Triton's pond.
I hear the snip-snap, the lone gardener clipping
a trellis rose. My pace quickens. The lone sundial
points toward home. I must hurry, make time
for the small café, the steamy espresso.

-- Jeanine Stevens

The Water Table – November

By now, the metal roof should be graced
with heavy frost,
      the needed storm only paltry.
Not an arborist, but I think ground water
sinks dangerously low.

Which direction are roots taking, so devoid
of moisture in yet another drought year.
Will they seek horizontal,
or tendril down hungrily gnawing
      to open pockets that hold nothing, voids
confused as everyone else.

I think of the pot-bound pink lemon you just planted
in deep earth, roots a tough spiral,
like a tightly woven basket,
      except
for one green stubborn shoot fingering
down through the ceramic hole—
seeking life. Reminds me of Dylan Thomas:

      "Force that through the green fuse
         drives the flower."

What if I've been planted in the wrong place
at the wrong time, wrong latitude, wrong century?
      Have I taken up too much space?

"Bloom Where You Are Planted," a popular
poster from the 1960's,
appreciated by some, disliked by others.

We are advised to look below the surface,
        not just skim the top
(which only works for clarifying butter).

                    -- *Jeanine Stevens*

Winter Arrives

Bare trees expose new sky and old nests
winter comes sweeping leaves into brown
piles, birds leave for the south, it's time
to sit on the ground again cold and alone.

The days shorten with a late sun rising pink
and icy, gulls fly high toward the coast,
I breathe white frost and ground fogs soak
my bed, another birthday brings winter.

Dark clouds build out west, threatening rain
over the tan washes cracked dry from summer.
I walk faster on numb feet, my head down
hands stiff, raw, looking for the road home.

-- Emily Strauss

Spring Coming

Grasses poke out of the snow banks
now, brown, dry, stiff from cold,
last year's remains hidden
for so long we must be reminded
of another season, one never
observed, taken on faith that snow
is not permanent here.

I should have guessed from unused
screens stacked in the closet,
netted hats, bug spray,
a log step to reach the bird feeder
buried in the snow pack,
mud boots, wooden slatted
walkways, clothes lines sagging
just above the frozen meadow,
a lawn chair hanging from a nail—

that there could be more than
pure white skirts around bare
trunks of poplar and birch,
muddy snow along the roads,
slick paths cut neatly down
with smooth, straight walls
up to my hips, roof topped
with clear crystal layers almost
geological.

I could almost take off
my hat today.

-- *Emily Strauss*

The First Rains

The rain fell through my sleep
all night until puddles gathered
in my dreams and I was ankle
deep in salty tidal pools—
the storm blew in hard gusts
slapping the wind chimes
hanging just outside my reach
until they clanged together
the tiny high notes mixed with
the deep bongs of long pipes

I heard them over the drain
spout rushing like old plumbing
flooding the dried rosemary
rooted where it would catch
every drop, a constant sound
that mixed with the dreaming
and blowing and pouring
until my sleep was soaked
limp like the juniper branches
washed green glistening, the dust

of summer finally washed away
now truly winter was raining—
my dreams became colder, damp
reflecting muddy paths dripping
from every brush of leaves, gray
clouds hanging low over the bed
a lid that held my visions low
over the streams now rushing by
old roots and my feet until I woke
gasping hard, nearly drowned.

-- Emily Strauss

Seasons

Spring

She is aureate smile of daffodil
as it awakens from winter-lorn siesta
on a crisp peppermint morn
after apparently scores of dawns,
draped in misted confusions.

The soft lilting rhapsody
of a skylark as it senses fragrance
in flowing realms of zephyr
and sings to welcome floral delights.

She is lingering sigh of sakura
which blossom in redolent brevity
~ haiku penned by nature's quill
on to be mouthed and scattered
in scented syllables
by a vociferous breeze.

Drizzling symphony of clouds
seeking to pepper petal-cheeks in gems-
as perfumed boudoir of Zephyrus,
enamors their vagrant souls.

Summer

Her laughter echoes in rippling gait
of cascading mountain brooks,
which flow down chiseled verdure
when a belligerent sun frowns.

She is infatuation
of a love-struck sunflower,
reiterating celestial path of Helios
with entranced gaze of one hypnotized.

She is fragrance of mango blossoms
which herald anticipations
of luscious, golden delights
soon to ripen on boughs of desire.

She is the elusive mirage
fleetingly cheating visions
on asphalted paths,
when light plays conjurer
on some harsh, perspiring noon.

Autumn

She is auburn whisper of nostalgia
withering from bony fingers
of geriatric mendicancy,
echoing on dusty trails
in cinnamon-scented ambiguity.

She is placid grin carved
on juicy melons of reality,
to concoct dancing shadows on
stark lamps of veracity.

She is the swiftness of squirrels
eagerly hoarding nuts,
only to be forgotten restart
another xylem-phloem equation,
while golden wheat-dreams ripen.

She is the mandarin moon
seen perched on nude branches,
delighting in the vista
of enceinte fields afore harvest.

Winter

She is the sepia morning,
apparently bleached of flavors and hues,
awakening lethargically to
steaming lure of caffeine~
seen through frosted panes
fingerprinted by wind's shivers.

She is warmth of blazing hearth
and blankets coaxing agility to laze,
on afternoons veiled in fog
while nostrils delight in scents
of roasted peanuts and brewed hot cocoa.

She the flavor of green peas
shelled in bowls like moments of leisure,
the aroma of greens permeating from
a kitchen's larder of allure.

She is the forbidden pleasure
of ice-creams savored in the chill
when snowflakes cover foliage rustles
like children after pillow tussles,
and fingers are numbly beg for sunshine.

-- *Smita Sriwastav*

I Am a Changing Dream . . .

I am chilled sigh
of blazing hearths of january,
scented in burnished whispers
from incinerated maple-wood,
and wafting warmth
from bittersweet cups
of frothy cappuccinos,
my veil spun by ancient hills
as translucent fogs,
my realms bejeweled in frost~
never tasted by
an anorexic, wizened sun.

I am confusion of february
a confluence of snowflake's monologues
and daffodils golden giggles,
cuddled in honeyed sunshine
reminiscent of lukewarm saffron milk
sweet, scented and mellow,
a moment dozing in time's grasp
forgotten as a caterpillar
nascent within its chrysalis
its butterfly flutters hibernating.

I am fragrance of march
exhaled by tulips,
the breath of lilacs hanging
as a divine promise
on thresholds of drowsy morns
I am withering hope of roses
marauded by spring showers,
exotic incense of orchids
wafting in sunshine,
psalms of worship echoing
from variegated lips
abloom in redolent meads.

I am the laughter of april,
reflected in sparkling gait
of a mischievous brook,
skipping on silver stilettos
on shingle scattered
like marbles in her path,
the days singed at corners
like marigold petals,
when winter slowly fades
with blankets cozying up
alongside moth ball piquancy
and summer blossoming
with flowers of mango trees.

I am the sultry breath of may,
with a sublime sun stealing
the chill from marble footsteps,
day like scribbled poetry~
a blend of shadows
and twilights strewn in
melodies strummed
on quixotic banjos of crickets,
while noons are parched words
thirsting for lemonades.

I am the clarity of june,
scented in ripeness of alphonsos,
molten serenade of distant blue hills
echoing in cascades
on velvet shod geometrics,
I am the rarity of china roses
speckled on verdure hedges,
my moments like acrylic graffiti splashed
rainbow wings worn by butterflies
writing sonnets in nectar.

I am the liquid treacle of july
poured over cobblestones

in silken symphonic fluidities,
the murmured epistles of
gypsy clouds writ in ripples
on muddy face of earth,
I am the bipolar moods of azure
an exuberant sunshine
mingling with grey overtones
of a mixed emotion tempest.

I am the whimsy
of august sunshine
oft enveloped
by monsoon clouds,
my chiaroscuro silences
tinted in tempest grays,
and trumpet of rowdy thunder,
with soft reverberations
of fluid melodies
brocaded on potholes
in musical ripples.

I am complacence of september
a subtle metamorphosis
molting myself in yellowed foliage,
an array of hours aromatic
with potpourri and flavored in
sweet gulps of apple cider,
a honeydew sun leniently smiling
over trail rustling in old songs,
and a butter bowl moon
perched on autumnal beggary,
as alms of benevolent, indigo skies.

I am brooding gaze of october
piled under boughs in tangerine,
tasting like crisp crackers
on the palate of consciousness,
I am a bronzed whisper

like baking cinnamon rolls,
my crepuscules withering in
burnt scales on indifferent roads,
mornings like placid hymns
reverberating in temples,
and nights like princess tiaras.

I am caress of november days
acronymed between elastic nights,
tinted in volatile golds
tasting like latte afternoons
flavored in sweet choco-chip cookies,
dew peppered salmon dawns,
scented in wisteria
and nights like lingering taste
of wine in crystal minutes,
with a muffler clad moon
pouring chianti on chilly soil.

I am snow-song on december
scattered in mute pearls on life,
my words muffled, my tune fractured
draping quietude in expectancy,
days like sepia reminiscences
from dogeared yester-years,
nights like forgotten emptiness
with a lazy moon asleep
under blankets of vague mists,
and stars reluctantly
grumbling on their long vigils,
trees adorned in silver jewels.

-- *Smita Sriwastav*

Spring

Bathed in nectar dew drops, now
the damsel spring stealthily
tiptoes into the hamlet
with all its strength.

The south breeze plays
fifth symphony on tender new leaves,
flings the grey garment of fugitive winter
on the tether of time.
The red modesty of cassia flowers
lazily thrown on the elevations,
sheuli flower hides her whitish face
in dark screen.
Forest being released from solitary confinement
bedecks with colors of nature
snow white swans conquest the copper sky
Jasmine frequently haunts dark nights.

The sun rises
on the forehead of a newlywed bride
as if it is a circular spot of vermilion.
Man in remaining incognito
for years, has come back
to the war fields of life,
perhaps he wants to pay
his debts of soul.

Somebody, in quest of a blue envelope
tinted with multicolor of unknown flowers
but the letter box of young heart
wide open, as the darkness of suspicion
has broken its lock,
the love knots of past love
lost in the time treacherous sand
anxiously asks for identity.

Still on the debris of sand castle
built of hopes and promises,
a young poet composes a lyric
with inks of blood and shades of despair
his pen of eternal pain proclaims,
"Spring has set in again
to solace thousands of broken hearts."

-- Neelamani Sutar

An Indian Summer

Summer greets the city
with glorious riots of color

Trees in full bloom
provide relief from rising mercury.

Nearing its peak,
summer brought
all its vices along with it,
but there's a certain reason
to cheer, for the city is
blooming again.

Alphabets of revolution
in the boughs of gold mohar,
African tulip and copper pod
are flames of forests.
Indian Laturnum, even Siamese Senna
or, they say
Red Cassia flowers,
blazing forest fire.

All these summer events
often called summer glories.
Red locket locks
are explosions of red buds
set fire on city road, gleaming.

Banaba plant puts forth blossoms
in young devastated minds,
now plays hide and seek
with the gentle south breezes.

Tender twigs welcome
the strange weather
with thousand clappings.

In his red hands,
a sublime fire,
though fearfully enchanting,
burns heavy hearts,
and young poets
torture them with unknown emotions.

The fire of flowers
may not burn the city life
but in the streets,
even flies swarm
to these red hot flowers,
burn themselves in pious lust.

-- Neelamani Sutar

Winter Solstice

White-washed winter meadow
ice-lace clings from every window
the grey veil of a lovely widow
torn to tears by the wind

Soaring icicle – needle piercing the snow
a yawing yew yearns for you
black crows creek
a lark moans its long lost love
holy berry bubbles like blood
the breath is a small smoke choke
heartbeat of a dark locomotive
immortality means dying constantly
The winter solstice turns the wheel of fortune
our willful solitude won't last long
resurrection tears the scenery to pieces

Spring comes with sunbeam – spears to kill
to kill winter boredom and
the dream of a
dormouse.

-- *Fanni Sütő*

The Poet Observes Quota Compliance, Take-Overs
and Net Capital Loss in Her Spring Garden

All through March and most of April,
the wind's been dancing daffodils to death
yellow dresses faded, folded, put away.

Now, it's May, and frowzy tulips
skirts half-off gossip
under cherry boughs pink, heavy
with blossom. Bluebells make more
of their bulbous babies underground
so that next year, next year
they can take over completely.

Calendulas with pretty much the same idea
pop up everywhere, last but a day or two
before they go to seed, repopulate the earth
with up-and-coming brilliants.
Robins squabble over worms,
the lilac's perfume pends.

The Crimson King sends seedpods
to the lawn, the wet stone steps.
Luscious dark red leaves unfold,
remain that way til June arrives
and caterpillars come
to turn those velvet leaves to lace.

-- Anne Swannell

Needles

Lights dim, come back to bright.
Windows rattle.
Thick blankets of snow laid down last night
wind now unravels, bullying its way
round the corner of the house,
shouldering through cedar boughs
a pastry chef who couldn't care less
where clouds of flour, unmeasured showers
of salt and sugar fall.

I'm on the couch, here in the warm,
mending my old denim jacket,
trying to make the stitches invisible,
cursing when my needle keeps unthreading.
The red plastic hummingbird feeder
suction-cupped to my window dips and dives
crimson coracle on a crazed ocean of air.

The Anna's Green's an iridescent mix
of sky and field and forest on the wing
brilliants that give the lie
to this bleached and bleaching fury.
I watch in admiration as he guides
his sipping needle through a bobbing eye.

-- Anne Swannell

Cyanocitta Cristata

My first sighting was in the oldest part of Trois-Rivières
one October. He was perched on a gite sign on rue des Urselines.
Out west, blue jays are much darker: Cyanocitta Stellaris.

It was the nearness, the crested lightness of him that cued me
to whip out my camera, but the sudden movement
sent him up onto the eaves below a dormered window,
where he began to chuck gobs of wet brown leaves
from the gutter to the ground—searching, I suppose,
for beetles, grubs, whatever chose to burrow there,
as if he knew they'd soon be under icy lock—no key.

I picture him now, in late December
as I fill the bird-feeder on my balcony
searching for scraps in the back gardens of rue des Ursulines—
the color of snow, of shadow on snow,
the color snow goes in gulley and ravine,
and in the ruts of driven roads.

-- Anne Swannell

The Ice Breakers

Excited voices echo in the Douglas firs;
has the lake really formed a skin
between itself and the new year ?
Christmas-scarf'd and toque'd,
children test the crystal shore
with tentative boots.
Tossed pebbles prove
how thick truth is.

Skipped stones touch, lift
and touch, skitter
into pure distance.

Where the lake enters the woods,
boys dig in their heels,
gouge out frozen pieces, hold them
up to the light,
shouting for the joy of being here
and dangerous in the unimagined afternoon.

Transported by a miracle
to the glassware department
Of Birks or The Bay,
they are dropping pieces of elegant crystal,
shattering fantastically valuable objects;
transparent plates and delicate goblets.

Soon they are shouldering
glittering chandeliers from the ceiling,
surrounded by mirrors that mirror them fearless
until even they are robbed of their vision.

Now the boys are climbing a rocky outcrop
overlooking the lake;
they begin to hurl stones, chunks of rock——
the biggest they can lift——
down to the lake's frosted surface.

The lake
creaks on its hinges.

Huge white bubbles
lurch upwards, inch
towards a quaking parallelogram——
a triangle, a hexagon——
any rocking window they can get to,
escape——elastic and silent——
into the diamond air.

The air is cooler now,
and bluer where the needles mass.
Toques removed in the heat of the attack
are pulled back on, scarves re-wrapped,
gloves exacted from pockets
for the long trek home.

Exhausted, each rock hurler
plunks in front of his television,
stares at the sullen surface,
activates the channel changer,
breaks the ice.

-- Anne Swannell

Listening to Ravel's Bolero While Two Leaves Spin Outside My Window

Back to back, suspended by a filament so thin
it's almost invisible against October's blue,

two curvaceous red-currant leaves spin.
Ravel dictates their every move,

building to a crescendo as each exotic twin
swivels, gyrates in a frenzy of ecstasy.

Like Mehmet the Conqueror's favorites,
they seem never to tire, clearly to know

there'll be difficulties if they do desist,
and when his fingers snap to tell them to.

                        -- *Anne Swannell*

The Holly Tree in Summer

In Celtic astrology, the holly is a summer sign:
the ruler presiding over the season
of strolling beneath full moons at midnight
and past the roaring lions carved from stone.

She herself thinks of this tree as
presiding over winter,
remaining green and glossy
when other trees are withered and bare,
offering clusters of red berries to
birds that remain in the north.

A holly grows in her neighbor's yard.
In summer, it does not preside
over the street as a maple does
or embrace mourners the way
that the oak at the Mt. Calvary cemetery will.

Knowing that she never strolls at midnight anymore
and the stone lions in her neighborhood
are cat-size forms worn down by summer rain,
she feels sympathy for this cramped tree
growing not on a mythical hillside in Ireland
but in this world and no other.

-- Marianne Szlyk

At the Almost-Empty Vegetarian Café

Prewar buildings cast long shadows on this October street,
blacking out yellow and orange leaves, the brilliant sky,
and her memories of marriage outside this city.

The clunk, whir, and grind of a carrot juicer
overwhelms the radio tuned to avoid
the silly love songs of American Top 40.

She wonders how long these shadows and sounds will continue.

Outside shadows melt into dusk the color of soy sauce and miso.
The man she intended to marry shepherds his children
into their building, the Cliff Dwelling over the river.
He will never stop here.

The man she did marry flies into this city tonight
with his new wife, his new Linda.
He will never stop here.

Only the young man nursing his tea, nursing his poetry,
living on half-price produce at home,
stops here.

Looking out to the almost-empty dining room,
she wonders how long all of this can go on.

-- Marianne Szlyk

***Sag Harbor, After a Long Habit of Turning Down Invitations
to Visit People in Their Summer Places***

I let the scoop
of gourmet ice cream fall
out of the cone.
An honest accident
on its own trajectory.
I didn't like the long line
pretending patience.
The well-heeled sandal crowd
wound around Sedutto's harbor side.
I gawked at grabby people
in front of me who could identify
their tastes. Their shorts,
their flip-flops, their blue-jean brands
and ice creams. After the contents
of my cone hit the ground
I refused a replacement,
I must have seemed pathetic
but I was frozen, stuck in argument
with the delicious beauty I had missed.

-- Susan Tally

What I Mean When I Say Ageless

When we met in the fall for the first time—
not as friends—the first time as possibility,
you were aging in reverse past twenty years,
some fresh-faced boy fumbling for admiration.
You brushed my arm. Shoulders press and retreat.
I secretly hoped we'd never find our way home.

But your father face returned—I met this man
many months before. We were friends
but so much older. Eyes heavy with marriage
and house and family and work responsibility.

When we met again for the first time—
past possibility, in the space of immediate now
where time is irrelevant and skin speaks
all our words, your face became child.
When I counted the spokes in your irises,
I looked down at the escaping years
dissolving through your teeth.

Let's be children in some night parking lot
without the weight of older lives.
We'll climb into ours beds as all time—
as delinquency—as heavy sage—
as eager limbs—as singing rosies round
and round, spinning into the music.

-- *Sarah Thursday*

When Winter Lingers Past the Solstice

It takes a skillful exorcist
to expel the cantankerous
cold heart of winter that lingers
past the solstice. March, a mere

amateur seminary student,
fails at this holy task, yielding
to late flurries that cancel
baseball games. Not so April—

powerful bright angel. She lashes
at winter with spikes of blue
and white delphiniums and shouts:
By the power of the god of renewal,

I command you abandon this place!
The old man limps away
on thin bones of melting ice,
muttering in his powdery voice.

-- Dennis Trujillo

Civil War

Bony branches grasp
at our coats as we suck
in lungfuls of peppermint breaths.

We hide in the white forest,
building a frozen castle
guarded by gingerbread soldiers.

War is coming, we say
as we stomp out a wide moat
and cake the walls with extra padding.

We gather jagged twigs
and plant them around our kingdom
for added protection.

Our cheeks burn red,
our Christmas gloves crackle
underneath layers of snow.

We top our construction
with a handmade flag, black and menacing
against the pale turrets.

But even as we hold tightly to each other,
waiting, we both know our castle will
fall with the thump of a gavel.

-- *Tesia Tsai*

Magnolias

Each Spring I wait for the magnolias
to throw their delicacy against
the hard brick city houses.

On upright branches, tiny
candle-buds, compact and sturdy
know they're on their way to flourish,
to unfold their secret scarf-like
petals, much as a conjuror keeps
hidden his best trick.

Now comes the time when
trees are heady, white or pink—
the white are always first—till
wind and rain, jealous of this
display, assault each branch, rip
fragile, skin-light fragments which
already turning brown, stick to the
wet dark pavements.

The tattered trees and I
await another Spring,
another flourishing.

-- Marion Turner

Watching from the Chair by the Window

We start this dance of fear in July
when the sun is building pyramids of heat.
Thursday, that limbo day we flatten our backs
without shimmying our way to the weekend.
Anxiety, a pair of bongo drums we beat
on the way to West Texas Oncology Center.

My stomach flinches, the nurse gloves up in latex,
connects the IV lines.
Chemo's cold ravages me from the inside.
Carol tucks a brown blanket beneath my feet,
plugs in the heating pad, sits in the chair by the window
where a seamless stream of light cascades.
We chat, place a bet on how long
it will take me to fall prey to sleep.
This is our ritual for a trinity of seasons,
lab work, doctors' appointments, chemo sessions.

From our window chairs,
we spend a myriad of Thursdays scrutinizing the sky.
October, we witness it cry apologetically all afternoon.
Its dull beam floods the day with wet sympathy.
January, we watch it explode with white.
Tiny crystal shards stick to streets, buildings, bald trees.
March, a blush of warmth fills its wide face.
A drowsy smile is edged in the angles of my mouth.
Carol wakes me from a Benadryl induced sleep,
snaps pictures of me with nurses and bobbing balloons.

Time burns through seconds
until they are heaped into a rubble of centuries.
We've been friends for less, but know how years
leap into that incessant flame.

-- Loretta Diane Walker

Telling Each Other They Are Loved Suppresses the Shudder

winter had brought the 0 degree
when you rode into Fargo
for your first treatment.

you asked out loud if it was cold
enough. there was nothing to say.

a month later
all that's left is colder
weather and the passing. there is no
need to leave the house
that overlooks the frozen lake
where you once grabbed a neighborhood boy
by the scarf before he fell through a hole
in the corner of the ice house.

anymore moments have depleted the remission
field from the source. you lie in bed.

mustering the strength
to talk on the phone
you want to know about the weather
here in California. the sun shines

while it sets in Minnesota. you ask
me to remember the stories
you have told. you wonder if you
have done well.

-- Toren Wallace

The Four Seasons

Anne and Jeremy lived
on the right side of Nuffield Ave
in a house painted wedgewood-blue
with white trimmed balconies

and a double garage where
their air-traffic-controller father
parked a new car each year,
even if he didn't really need one.

Some afternoons their mother
dressed up to drink dry sherry,
fold the shawl away and play Vivaldi
on the grand piano in the bow window

near the roses. She always got stuck
in Autumn.

-- Mercedes Webb-Pullman

Seasons of Love

When he comes to you in the morning
he is fresh; spring breeze in wheat,
green growth of vine and leaf.
Together you entwine.

When he comes at midday
he is golden heat
haze over paddocks
without shadows.
Together you abound.

When he comes in evenings
he is welcome warmth;
red glow of apples,
embers in a banked fire.
Together you are harvest.

When he comes for you in the night
he is a cold black mirror.
He will take you once;
it will be forever.
Together you'll make winter.

-- *Mercedes Webb-Pullman*

Making a Poem #7

Pendant clusters glow, exposed
along the snaky vine whose
leaves have succumbed
to autumn. Today

winter's first frost has etched
silver filigrees over each globe;
instructions in a secret script
of fruit so you know it's time

to gather the grapes, press them
barefoot so they all blend, ecstatic
in this ancient alchemy, memories
of the year compressed into this.

Time to distill spring's green shoots
with gold of summer honey bee's
drowsy buzzing, replete, steep these
in autumn orange warmth suspended

until this freezing morning breathed
the fatal transmigration's
final touch; fire of ice refines
the true elixir, ambrosial Eiswein.

-- Mercedes Webb-Pullman

Winter Walk

The chimes tinkle outside
my bedroom window this Sunday night
at the end of a year,
my gratitude an unopened box.
I tear at the wrapping to reveal
the gifts inside: a full moon,
a soft winter night walk,
a kiss so long in coming I am
surprised at the suddenness,
your hand soft in mine,
strange and right. No fear welled up
in my heart, its beat slow and steady.
I don't miss the wild waves
of a heart crashing on rocks and sand.

                              -- *Mary L. Westcott*

Secret Stache

I store summers
under a wide maple tree
buried for the day I shovel
them into sunlight

dirt   pebbles tossed
until I hit my buried
cache of sunlight
to tremble in warm winds

my hoarded skies
breach darkness to billow
high above glazed eyes
and confound this cold earth

-- Joanna M. Weston

Gardener's Return

I come home to breaking buds
petals stretching yellow curves
while bees orchestrate
a zinging symphony
from overture to *adagio*
under bird chorus *forte*
my footsteps the drumbeat
of a fanatic gardener

fingers ache to dip
honeyed soil and give
seeds seeds seeds
where worms congregate
enriching organic growth
when summer bends to heat

-- Joanna M. Weston

One Clean Sheet

pegged damp   heavy
to the washing line

blown to fullness
by a sunlit wind

then corner by corner
I fold   soft   dry

place in the cupboard
with lavender

wait for Saturday
when together we

change used-for-a-week
to the mattress

snap scented edges
across a king-size

stretch then tuck
one blanket on top

to know solstice heat
held in our dreams

scented by summer
day into night

-- Joanna M. Weston

Winter Argument

Alright Winter, you hoary Bitch
you know I don't like you
& I suspect you don't care
much about me either. But
I've always tried to play fair.
You're outside & I'm inside.
I don't like bonfires in the backyard
or dance around my porch blasting
a hair-dryer to drive you away.
Well, maybe sometimes I build a fire
in the fireplace, the rising smoke
pushing you back from the chimney.
But you always return the next morning.
The deal is you have the outside
I pull the lined curtains closed
turn up the heat, drink hot coffee.
I have the inside

Now I see that you are creeping
into my house, not my bedroom
not my kitchen, but *My Room*
where I'm surrounded by books
by music, pens, my notebooks.
The ominous stains on the ceiling
the lines like tears on my wall
tell me you are licking your way in
to remind me of your ice & snow
on my roof, tell me I'm not safe
that some day you will come crashing
in laughing that icy cackle, shivering
with vicious, cold-hearted joy.

If you're going to do it, be quick.
The Ground Hog tells me your days

are numbered & my girls, the crocus
& lilacs are just waiting to push you away.

-- Dan Wilcox

Grandmother Spider Sews the Fabric of Seasons Together

My Grandmother Spider climbed a web
into the sky when she died. She went through
the Forth World of the Hopi, sewed the clouds
together so none of the Star People could tumble
out by accident. She wrote in the sky messages
using herons. If I could read these signs,
it would keep me in practice of the old ways
as well as tell me, all currents of the winds
are for canoes, all rain drops are ancestors
memories, all seasons are stitches of a blanket,
all thunder clouds are buffalo stampeding.

Grandmother, I still speak the true language
as well as the dream-talking. When summer
is warm, it is for planting, for riding backwards,
for catching fish barehanded. When winter
comes out of her tipi, wearing bear-skin robes
white as bared chattering teeth, turning her head
around like a snowy owl, she asks where you are,
why you are not swapping stories during
the long months when all life moves slow and sure.
When spring rides on coyote, dressed in flowers,
and dragging in the sun for everyone to eat,
I remember the good pipe smoke after,
how you made your own from a branch
saying it feel for you to use and you saw it
once in a vision, like a crane's leg.
When fall lumbers away, tired of arguing
with the next season, tired of all berries
not returning, snarling like a kicked dog,
he does not want to talk about the old days.

Grandmother, I hold onto all the stories,
all the secrets of seeds, all the ways to read
clouds and water currents, our language,
like they were skin, like laughter

from locust, like rattling bones.
As long as I hold onto these webs
tangled around me, we can continue
to talk like this whenever I need.

-- *Martin Willitts, Jr.*

Bird Charm
  sorbus ancuparia

With the reddish fall
of rowen leaves
piled into a ruckus,

the lance of another year almost gone,
small shoulders and her arms
raking, her purpose had been

to tumble back into living—
small apples, aromatic
bark burning, thickets

of waxwings—to shake free
the bitter ashes. She carried it all
to beds dormant with sage,

thyme, and lemon balm,
shredded and scattered
into a layer against the snows

they stood watching that winter.
They could hold her. They couldn't
heal her. Charming, healing, the stars
were skills I could try to learn.

I can be their female-Merlin,
Niniane, Morgan—boughs, isle of apples,
tire swings, climbing trees, heartwood.

When the dowsing rod pauses,
the foliage of fruit, the fragrant
inner bark, I study the tricks of bird lime.

                    -- Laura Madeline Wiseman

Pippin

Unbuttoning her coat beyond the blush
of russet red. She shivers in whispers:
the seeded core browning in frosted light.

-- Phil Wood

Appalachian Spring

From this highest point, no real horizon:
the Smokies' tree-softened jags slide upwards
until indistinguishable from the thin grey

terpene-laden haze. At our feet, sunlight
picks out from coniferous green those gnarled
arthritic branches whose writhe has become set

in the rigidity of death. The shadow
of our spindly tower, stretching westward
across the randomly-dying firs, zigzags

abruptly up and over the dazzling spiral slope
up which we'd walked. So very different
from where we'd begun, down in the V

of some exuberant tributary of the Cherokee,
under sunlit cumuli of freshly-broken green
where swallowtails were flittering, uncertain

as yellowed leaves of where they'd rest,
while testing the zephyrous air for hints
of females quivering on the dappled earth.

Up here the insects are less flamboyant, creeping
unnoticed in the grain of the bark, divining
with ichneumon skill just where to drill for sap

and dribble death. A lifetime on, I guess,
a few firs will still be standing, proud of a bald,
intransigent snags to the whim of the wind.

                    -- *Mantz Yorke*

*Note: The balsam woolly adelgid is an aphid-like insect that attaches
itself to the bark of the Fraser fir. Toxin is injected from its saliva
whilst sucking sap. Infested trees die within a few years. The insect
was discovered in the Great Smoky Mountains ("the Smokies") in
1963.*

The Blossoming, Kopelovo, 1986

In the orchard, the breaking
of pinkish buds. The horizon,
once distant through winter twigs,
has drawn in, a stippled ring
of green and apple-white. Light

is falling through the branches
of a chestnut, dappling shadows
on a grey-green tent and the patient
queue shuffling forward in the hot
pollen-dusty air. Here

white-coated orderlies welcome us
with curious words, microphones
crackle like radio static
and syringes gorge themselves
on our blood. All is well,

they tell us; we'll go home soon,
when the petals are lying white
upon the ground. We can't yet tell
the wind-blown pollen's struck,
and fruits have begun to swell.

-- Mantz Yorke

Snowscape, River Usk

Low tide. Beneath the bridge the muddy bank
has become the Himalayas, white ribs and spurs
jutting like dendrites from the gullied ooze.

This first half-inch of snow has defined precisely
the frozen writhe of oaks I'd barely noticed earlier
against drab grass. Further back a copse –

yesterday, a flattish fuzz – is fading grainily,
plane by plane, into the indeterminate
monotone of falling snow. Softly, evening

is settling save where yellowed hay, unmown
near the scribbly tangle of bramble-wire,
stabs from the snow its shocks of chrome.

-- Mantz Yorke

Seasonal Stanzas

Spring: like a raindrop
on a small lotus leaf
unable to find the spot
to settle itself down
in an early autumn shower
my little canoe drifts around
near the horizon
beyond the bare bay

Summer: in her beehive-like room
so small that a yawning stretch
would readily awaken
the whole apartment building
she draws a picture on the wall
of a tremendous tree
that keeps growing
until it shoots up
from the cemented roof

Autumn: not unlike a giddy goat
wandering among the ruins
of a long lost civilization
you keep searching
in the central park
a way out of the tall weeds
as nature makes new york
into a mummy blue

Winter: after the storm
all dust hung up
in the crowded air
with his human face
frozen into a dot of dust
and a rising speckle of dust
melted into his face
to avoid this cold climate

of his antarctic dream
he relocated his naked soul
at the dawn of summer

-- *Changming Yuan*

Summerscape

The galley of an unknown author's work
In a fully justified format:
Every stark hill italicized
Every glaring lake capitalized
With no single tree misspelled
Or single flower misplaced

Again and yet again, the sun has
Proofread the text
With all its attention

And
Found everything just ready to go

-- *Changming Yuan*

Autumnscape

between two sharp chest ribs
    of an isolated birch skeleton
        dusk-dyed and wind-carved
    hung still on an invisible wall
comes to perch an ageing crow
    whose bold beak holds a cold
        and pale prophesy old
    with all withered leaves palette-cut
blowing towards gates and doors
    like the fliers sent randomly
        from an alien chain store

        -- Changming Yuan

Winterscape

so little triggers
off

a black bird
the nexus of antithesis
foiled with snow
light

to fly into the vast history of
gray

-- Changming Yuan

From The Editors

Walking with Wings

February beaches belong to the birds. They congregate
like conventioneers, squawking bitterly about the trials
of flight. The older ones moan. Migration gets harder
every year, though the warm southern winds do soothe
their tired joints. The younger ones battle waves,
race to see who can capture the first fish, back peddle
when angry tides decide they have had enough.
New mothers struggle to track their fledglings. Beginning
takeoffs sputter, end in splashdowns. Undiscouraged,
feathers are shaken dry, prepared for the next attempt.
A bicycle dares trespass, entire sky flutters for just a moment,
echoes with warnings and protests. As it passes, plumes
resettle, beaks turn to stare after it with unmasked disdain.

-- A.J. Huffman

An Unscheduled Change in Persona

Spring knocked on my window
yesterday, and my closet erupted
with petals. Potential was in
the air, and I was afraid
I had cut growing optimism short
when I tripped over three packages
I did not remember buying. The first
held boxing gloves, which made sense
as I was always at war with something.
The second held water balloons,
but no hint of a target. Perplexed,
I dug through the third, which
appeared to be empty. Then I remembered
I bought a pound of peace at the farmer's
market—a good deal—as I traded it
for three faulty magic beans. I originally had
five, but I planted two outside my window,
waited weeks for a shoot
to send me into the clouds. Like always,
the flower that grew fell short of expectation,
but would, I now saw, make
an excellent accessory for last year's blouse.

-- *A.J. Huffman*

Lake Huron Rocks

resonate under foot. Miniature rainbows
of tone and texture fight for surface. Time
is their testimony. They have survived
extreme seasonal onslaughts, only to roll
over, allow the next pebble a moment's perch,
secure that this newcomer is not a replacement,
but an additional highlight to their show.

-- *A.J. Huffman*

The Path

as yet untaken, shows itself in white.
Pristine snow drips from sheltering branches.
I hesitate, hoping to maintain
this untouched scene a moment longer
before crushing crystals beneath excited feet
that cannot wait to see where it will lead.

-- A.J. Huffman

Spring Released

> -- *after* Born To Fly *by Vladamir Kush*

its hold on the candle's flame, but the strange
flickering form did not whisper away into tendrils
of dissipating smoke. It had been watching
the world through the paned glass of the living
room window and realized finite was a concept
for more foolish minds and less malleable bodies.
So beneath a transitory moon it began to forge
itself a shell . . . Wick . . . became stem . . . took root
branched out . . . opened . . . to embrace brittle skin
that smiled back, a reflection of a beautiful beginning,
but still not enough . . . Leaf . . . broke . . .
                                    fell . . .
refused to touch ground . . . fluttered . . . became wing
divided . . . synced stroke . . . took flight . . . changed
the world . . . as it erupted, a wintery bullet built
from the wishes of wax and glass.

> -- *A.J. Huffman*

I Am Leaf

lingering limb, a testament
to greener memories. I am holding
vigil against chilling winds'
strengthening force. I am withering
straggler, refusing to release
last tethering touch. I am
finger of spring, slipping.
I am fall
        ing, floating,
                softly drifting
into season's sleep.

-- A.J. Huffman

Daily Downpour

I can tell time by the force
of the rain. It is summer
in Florida, and the sky
has turned against us. Evil
clouds creep in at dawn, gray
bulging bellies already threatening
to birth another deluge,
but release is restricted
until noon, when the first trickling
tears escape. Once
the seal is broken, progression is swift.
Angrier bursts explode at hourly intervals
until the evening. Sunset brings stinging
sideways torrents, angrily battering closed
windows, threatening to break
fragile glass. By midnight,
something has been tempered,
drizzling tendrils squeeze themselves from self-
sealing cracks in evaporating layer of hovering
shadows. The pre-dawn hours sizzle,
stem as humidity rises with steam
from sidewalks trying to burn themselves
dry, in preparation for tomorrow's precipitating
drops.

-- A.J. Huffman

The Signs of Spring

Pollen dancing on wind—
yellow mist of promise,
tomorrow's kiss, landing, waiting
to be born again as petal, brush,
tree. A shift in temperament—
warmer air descending, a blanket
of energy, opening invisible arms
in welcome, a nudge to discard
shell-like coverings, to emerge
as butterfly with wings at the ready.
A dash of raindrops—
final blessing, tears of passage,
winter's last dissolve, expunged
as gentle fingers, a stroking
of magic, molecules of iridescent blue
christening green.

-- A.J. Huffman

The Cold Hand of Winter

has left my heart hollow.
I ache for warmth—
touch of sun, kiss of rain,
simmering breath of Spring.
Budding flame, my body
begs to be swallowed by green
rebirth. I bloom
with hope, grow with every bursting
seed, every upturned petal and leaf.

-- A.J. Huffman

December, 2013

It is the age of crow's feet and Botox, a battle
between chronology and discovery
of how old I do not feel. Today it is five
miles on treadmill, tomorrow, arthritic
knees, carpal tunnel. All syndromes and no sun.
December is the longest month, the cruelest,
save April and ice thawing. Yesterday, sheets
of snow fell on cars in Dallas, whole rooftops
losing their winter white like false hope.
In Pennsylvania, this was not newsworthy, filler
because everyone had caught enough glimpses
of Mandela lying in state. Nothing belongs to us,
not the failures or the empty bartering we do
in bed some nights when we are willing
to trade sleep for something that feels
a little more like awake.

-- *April Salzano*

Goodbye September

with your late illusion
of summer, your incessant transitions,
your morning fog.
You have been a month
of Monday's, a bitch of a beginning,
a hell of an end.

-- *April Salzano*

It's Just What We Do (Winters Up North)

Some days are so cold we put all the clothes
we own on our backs at once. We wear snow
boots for five months out of the year,
sport animal hides and pelts for reasons
of practicality. We always take extra
time to get anywhere, then sometimes don't
because we can't, but not because we didn't
try, despite weather advisories. We incessantly
squirt windshield washer fluid (both front and back
windows) to clear the slush, wash our cars
in the snow to combat the salt that's eating
our paint. We walk with our head down
to hide from the wind and rush
because we are cold, not because we are rude,
though we do have short fuses. We buy
staples before the storm, just in case,
and are usually surprised we made
it through another one. We talk a lot
about the weather, but we do not stop
for any of it. We stoke the fire
then spread the ashes on the ice, shovel
the snow, and start all over again tomorrow.

-- April Salzano

For One Son

I've got French fries, grease baked on, curling
against themselves as if they are unaware
of teeth and jaw. For the other son,
fallen leaves to rake and criticism, because twelve
is an age that needs both. For my husband,
I bear witness from the bathroom window.
He does not know I saw him as he flipped
the picnic table to find it dry rotted, collapsible
like a child's toy version of lawn furniture.
He raised his right hand and dropped it
at his side, mouthing what he would have said
if a car had pulled out in front of him. The table
should have fallen apart on someone
else's watch. Firewood. Winter left today,
but is coming back tomorrow. How can it
go from 64 degrees to -7 in less than 24
hours? I am in short sleeves, pale and neglected
though I have wintered in domestic heat for months.

-- April Salzano

Smelling God

after the rain-washed ground,
the scent of mud and minnows,
but I am nowhere
near a lake. In a circle
of pines, smoke.
Olfaction of light becomes
possible here, an offering
of self and skin.

-- April Salzano

Smelling Stinkbug

Shop vac vs. insect, stench
winning regardless of victor.
The brown triangles are alive, fat
with odor, antennae peering
over curtain rod, legs poking
from gathered valance. Why
they gravitate toward the Freon
of the window A/C unit is beyond
me. The way in or the way out?
Inside the canister of my weapon,
they have survived. I know this
the way I know their eggs
have been left behind,
the way I know summer is over.

-- *April Salzano*

I Am Going to Kick April's Ass

The month's, not my own,
if months have body parts,
which I am pretty sure they do
since I know I heard March
tell me to suck its dick.

-- April Salzano

July and My Mother's Twin

are both dead, closed forever like a lockbox
we lost the key for. My mother
says since birth she has always felt something
was missing, like she should have a third arm,
just as she has three kidneys. I imagine
a fat bean swimming in thick, red chili,
a division down its middle, chambering it
into the simplest dichotomy:
functioning and non. August is here.
The heaviest month arrives like a pair of bare
breasts waiting for let down. Only one
needs to be uncovered. The other must wait
like the hungry mouth of a stillborn,
gaping in a humid pocket of summer.

-- April Salzano

The Day Was Buried

Under a mound of fresh dirt,
worms make new tunnels to the roots
of flowers my husband planted,
the latest in an effort to erase
a spring that would not give way
to the brighter blooms of summer.

-- *April Salzano*

Author Bios

Jonel Abellanosa resides in Cebu City, the Philippines. His poetry has appeared or is forthcoming in numerous journals, including *The McNeese Review, Anglican Theological Review* and *Pedestal* (United States), *The Ofi Press* (Mexico), *Poetry Pacific* (Canada), *Deep Water Literary Journal* (Ireland), *Allegro Poetry Magazine* (United Kingdom), *The Bangalore Review* (India), *Poetry Kanto* (Japan), *Cha* (Hong Kong), *Eastlit* (Thailand), *Otoliths* (Australia), *Anak Sastra* (Malaysia), *New Verse News* (Indonesia), *Lontar* (Singapore). His poetry has been selected for the 2015 *Dwarf Stars Anthology* of the Science Fiction Poetry Association. He has a chapbook, *Pictures of the Floating World (Kind of a Hurricane Press,* United States). He is working on two full length collections, *Multiverse* and *100 Acrostic poems.*

Trevor Alexander is a retired Chemical Engineer living in Bradford, West Yorkshire in the UK. Born in Belfast, he moved to the UK to study and to escape the Troubles in Northern Ireland in the 60s & 70s. After a lifetime working in the chemical industry he has taken up writing in retirement, and is currently exploring various poetic forms.

Kara Arguello was born and raised in Pittsburgh, Pennsylvania, and now lives, works and writes in San Jose, California. Her work has appeared in *Cream City Review, The Fourth River, Sugar House Review,* and *Aperçus Quarterly*, among others.

Carol Alena Aronoff is a Ph.D., is a psychologist, teacher and writer who co-founded SAGE, a psycho-spiritual program forelders, helped guide a Tibetan Buddhist Meditation center, taught Eastern spirituality and healing practices; imagery, meditation, and women's health at San Francisco State University. She guided Healing in Nature retreats in Hawaii and the southwest, and had a counseling practice in Marin County for many years. She co-authored "Practical Buddhism: The Kagyu Path" with Ole Nydahl in 1989 and edited five books and four meditation booklets on Tibetan Buddhism. Dr. Aronoff published a textbook: "Compassionate Healing: Eastern Perspectives" in 1992. Her poetry has been published in Comstock Review, Potpourri, Poetic Realm, Poetica, Mindprints, Dream Fantasy International, Beginnings, Hawaii Island Journal, In Our Own Words, Theater of the Mind, Animals in Poetry, From the Web, HeartLodge, Out of Line, Sendero, Buckle&, Iodine, Asphodel, Tiger 's Eye, Nomad's Choir, Cyclamens & Swords, The New Verse News, and Avocet. She received a prize in the 1999/2000 Common Ground spiritual poetry contest, judged by Jane Hirshfield, and is a Pushcart Prize nominee. She won the Tiger's Eye contest on the writing life and has participated a number of times in Braided Lives, a collaboration of artists and poets as well as in SKEA's Art and Nature event, Ekphrasis: Sacred Stories of the Southwest, and (A) Muses Poster Retrospective for the 2014 Taos Fall Arts Festival. She was judge for the 2008 Tiger's Eye poetry contest. A chapbook of Native American/Hawaiian poems, Cornsilk, was published by Indian Heritage Council in 2004, and her illustrated poetry book, The Nature of Music, was published by Pelican Pond in 2005. An expanded, illustrated Cornsilk was published in 2006, Her Soup Made the Moon Weep, in 2007 and Blessings from an Unseen World in 2013. Currently, Dr. Aronoff resides in a rural area of Hawaii--working her land, meditating in nature and writing

Allen Ashley previously appeared in *A Touch of Saccharine* and *Life Is A Roller Coaster*. He writes regularly for the British Fantasy Society's "Journal" and "Newsletter". He works as a writing tutor in north London, UK, running five groups, including Clockhouse London Writers. His most recent books are, *Sensorama: Stories of the Senses,* as editor (Eibonvale Press, 2015) and *Dreaming Spheres: Poems of the Solar System* co-written with Sarah Doyle and published by PS Publishing (UK) in 2014. He has just finished guest-editing an issue of the online magazine *Sein und Werden* with the theme "The Restless Consumer."

Michael Ashley is a thirty-something 9-to-5er, plodding his way through life. He resides in the UK in the county of West Yorkshire, in his spare time he enjoys walking his dogs, and also writes a little. He is currently an editor at www.poetrycircle.com

Steve Ausherman has been thrice nominated for the Pushcart Prize in poetry and has been included in numerous literary magazines and online publications. His first chapbook of poetry entitled, *Creek Bed Blue* (Encircle Publications, 2012), was a finalist for a 2014 New Mexico Book Award and celebrates family, farming and a connection to place. His second chapbook entitled *Marking the Bend* (Encircle Publications, 2015) explores the grounding and transformative aspects of travel. His work has recently been included in the poetry anthologies Switch (The Difference), Mo' Joe, Petals in the Pan, and Voices of New Mexico III. Free time finds him exploring the trails and backroads of the American West with his wife Denise.

Donna Barkman was born into a family of actors, and started performing in kindergarten and has been writing for a dozen years. Recent productions: "What Goes Around" and a solo play, "Sticks and Stones and Women's Bones," produced in NYC and Peekskill, NY. Her poetry has been published in The Westchester Review, Pennsylvania English, Chautauqua, Common Ground, Adrienne Rich: A Tribute Anthology, and others. She's enjoyed two artist residencies in Wyoming.

Emily Bartholet is a high school senior as of spring, 2015. Following graduation, she will attend Dickinson College and is yet to decide on a major. Emily's poetry, prose, and photography have been published in magazines including *Teen Ink* and *The Riveter Review*. She re-founded a literary magazine at her school, enjoys blogging for *The Stardust Gazette*, and plans on participating on the staffs of several college publications.

Jonathan Beale has appeared regularly in Decanto, Penwood Review, The Screech Owl, Danse Macabre, Danse Macabre du Jour, Poetic Diversity, and also; Voices of Israel in English, MiracleEzine, Voices of Hellenism Literary Journal, The Journal, Ink Sweat & Tears, Down in the Dirt, & (Drowning: Down in the Dirt July 13) The English Chicago Review, Mad Swirl, Poetry Cornwall, Leaves of Ink, Ariadne's Thread, Bijou Poetry Review, Calvary Cross, Deadsnakes Review, The Bitchin Kitsch, The Dawntreader, I am not a Silent Poet, Pyrokinection,

Festival of Language, 'Don't Be Afraid: An Anthology to Seamus Heaney' and Ygdrasil. He was commended in Decanto's and Café writers Poetry Competitions 2012. And is working on a collection for Hammer and Anvil. He studied philosophy at Birkbeck College London and lives in Surrey England.

Colin Bell published his first novel, *Stephen Dearsley's Summer Of Love*, October 2013 by Ward Wood Publishing. It was long-listed for the Polari Prize 2014. His second, Blue Notes, Still Frames, will be published in 2016 (Ward Wood Publishing). He was a producer-director of arts documentaries and then Executive Producer, Music and Arts at Granada Television, making arts programs for ITV, BBC and Channel Four. His television credits include Celebration, God Bless America, My Generation, Menuhin's Children and It Was Twenty Years Ago Today. His poetry has been published in the UK and the USA by The Blotter, Cinnamon Press, Soaring Penguin Press, Muse-pie Press, Every Day Poets, Kind Of A Hurricane Press and Bittersweet Editions. He lives in Lewes, UK, and is currently working on his third novel.

Nina Bennett is a Delaware native and the author of *Sound Effects* (2013, Broadkill Press Key Poetry Series). Her poetry has appeared in numerous journals and anthologies including *Napalm and Novocain, Reunion: The Dallas Review, Houseboat, Yale Journal for Humanities in Medicine, Philadelphia Stories,* and *The Broadkill Review*. Awards include 2014 Northern Liberties Review Poetry Prize, second-place in poetry book category from the Delaware Press Association (2014), and a 2012 Best of the Net nomination. Nina is a founding member of the TransCanal Writers.

Stefanie Bennett has published several volumes of poetry and had poems appear with *Mad Swirl, The Camel Saloon, Illya's Honey, Jelly Fish Whispers, Shot Glass Journal, Boston Poetry Magazine* and others. She has acted as a publishing editor and worked with Arts Action for Peace. Of mixed ancestry [Italian/Irish/Paugussett-Shawnee] she was born in North Queensland, Australia, in 1945. Stefanie's latest poetry collection *The Vanishing* [Walleah Press] is available online from Walleah Press, Amazon and Fishpond.

Karen Berry lives and works in Portland, Oregon. Her poetry has appeared in numerous publications throughout the United States and Canada. Her first novel, *Love and Mayhem at the Francie June Memorial Trailer Park*, was published in 2014.

Suzette Bishop teaches at Texas A&M International University in Laredo, Texas, and is a contributing editor for Stockport Flats Press. She has published three books of poetry, *Hive-Mind*, *Horse-Minded*, and *She Took Off Her Wings and Shoes*, and a chapbook, *Cold Knife Surgery*. Her poems have appeared in many journals and in the anthologies *Imagination & Place: An Anthology*, *The Virago Book of Birth Poetry*, and *American Ghost: Poets on Life after Industry*. A poem from her first book won the *Spoon River Poetry Review* Editors' Prize Contest. In addition to teaching, she has given workshops for gifted children, senior citizens, writers on the US-Mexico border, at-risk youth, and for an afterschool arts program serving a rural Hispanic community.

Jane Blanchard lives and writes in Georgia. Her work has recently appeared in *Light*, *Slant*, and *U.S.1 Worksheets*.

Larry Blazek was born in Northern Indiana,but I moved to the southern part because the climate is more suited to cycling and the land is cheap.He has been publishing the magazine-format collage *Opossum Holler Tarot* since 1983 and could use some submissions. He has been published in the *The Bat Shat, Vox Poetica, Leveler Poetry, Five Fishes, Front* and *Mountain Focus Art* among others.

Irene Bloom is an emerging poet from Seattle, Washington whose work is inspired by her world travels, love of language, and sharing the written word with others. Her poems have appeared in Poetry Super Highway, Drash Northwest Mosaic, Voices Israel ,and the Poetry Box. She received an honorable mention for her poem *The Carrier* in the Reuben Rose Poetry Competition, published in the 2014 Voices Israel Anthology.

Barbara Brooks is the author of two chapbooks: "The Catbird Sang" and "A Shell to Return to the Sea," and is a member of Poet Fools. Her work has been accepted in *Avalon Literary Review, Chagrin River Review, The Foundling Review, Blue Lake Review, Granny Smith Magazine, Third Wednesday, Shadow Road Quarterly, Indigo Mosaic Muddy River Poetry Review, Boston Literary Magazine* and on line at *Southern Women's Review, Poetry Quarterly, Big River Poetry, Agave Magazine* among others. She currently lives in North Carolina with her dog.

Michael H. Brownstein has been widely published throughout the small and literary presses. His work has appeared in *The Café Review, American Letters and Commentary, Skidrow Penthouse, Xavier Review, Hotel Amerika, Free Lunch, Meridian Anthology of Contemporary Poetry, The Pacific Review, Poetrysuperhighway.com* and others. In addition, he has nine poetry chapbooks including *The Shooting Gallery* (Samidat Press, 1987),*Poems from the Body Bag* (Ommation Press, 1988), *A Period of Trees* (Snark Press, 2004), *What Stone Is* (Fractal Edge Press, 2005), *I Was a Teacher Once* (Ten Page Press, 2011), *Firestorm: A Rendering of Torah* (Camel Saloon Press, 2012) and *The Katy Trail, Mid-Missouri, 100F Outside and Other Poems* (Kind of Hurricane Press, 2012). . He is the editor of *First Poems from Viet Nam* (2011). Brownstein taught elementary school in Chicago's inner city (he is now retired), but he continues to study authentic African instruments, conducts grant-writing workshops for educators, designs websites and records performance and music pieces with grants from the City of Chicago's Department of Cultural Affairs, the Oppenheimer Foundation, BP Leadership Grants, and others.

Tanya Bryan is a Canadian writer with work published in Latchkey Tales, Feathertale Review, and Longest Hours - thoughts while waiting anthology. She loves to travel, writing and drawing her experiences, which are often surreal and wonderful. She can be found @tanyabryan on Twitter.

Wayne F. Burke has appeared in *Lost Coast Review, American Tanka, Bluestem, Dirty Chai, The Commonline Journal, Forge Journal, Fish Food Magazine,* and elsewhere. His book of poems, *Words that Burn,* is published by Bareback Press (2013). A second book of poems, *Dickhead*, is scheduled for publication by Bareback in June, 2015.

Miki Byrne began performing her poetry in a Bikers Club. She has had three collections of poetry published and work included in over 160 respected poetry magazines and anthologies. Miki has won poetry competitions and been placed in many others. She has read on both Radio and TV and judged poetry competitions. She was a finalist for Gloucester Poet Laureate. Miki is a member of the charity Arthritis Care's People Bank. She has been disabled for many years.

Janet Rice Carnahan lives in La Jolla, California with her husband, Bruce, a retired physicist. Originally from Santa Cruz, California, Janet comes from a large family and has two adult children and one grandson. Her education, including a Master's degree, was in early childhood education, human development and family studies. Janet has been published in many online journals and in three anthologies. She also has one caption and a cover photo to her credit. Her other interests include traveling, walking on the beach, photography, metaphysics and healing work. Janet's web site, "Hear Earth Heart" explores some of these topics and offers her four self-published poetry books.

Alan Catlin has been publishing for decades now. Some days he feels like The Ancient of Days, other days, like The Old Man and the Sea. His latest anticipated collection of poetry is *Last Man Standing* from Lummox sometime in 2015.

Aidan Clarke has been a writer for more than 3 decades during most of which he has lived, worked and walked around in Newcastle Upon Tyne. He has been performing his poetry at Spoken Word events for 4 years. His USP is a menu of around 140 poems each of which he can perform off by heart on request.

Sharon Cote is an Associate Professor of English and English Linguistics at James Madison University in Harrisonburg, VA, where she teaches various linguistics courses and science fiction.

She sees obvious connections between these two studies. She loves language, both for its infinite potential and for its quirky rules, and her current scholarly work focuses on metaphor.

Chella Courington is a writer and teacher. She's the author of three flash fiction chapbooks along with three chapbooks of poetry. Stories and poetry have appeared in numerous anthologies and journals including *SmokeLong, The Los Angeles Review, Nano Fiction,* and *The Collagist.* Her recent novella, *The Somewhat Sad Tale of the Pitcher and the Crow* (Pink.Girl.Ink.Press), soon will be available at Amazon. Born and raised in the Appalachian south, she now lives in Santa Barbara, CA, with another writer and two cats.

Linda M. Crate is a Pennsylvanian native born in Pittsburgh yet raised in the rural town of Conneautville. Her poetry, short stories, articles, and reviews have been published in a myriad of magazines both online and in print. Recently her two chapbooks *A Mermaid Crashing Into Dawn* (Fowlpox Press, June 2013) and *Less Than A Man* (The Camel Saloon, January 2014) were published. Her fantasy novel *Blood & Magic* was published in March 2015.

Wayne Cresser is a professor of English at Dean College. He lives on an island in Narragansett Bay with his wife and pup. Most recently his fiction has been published in the print anthologies Motif 1-3 (Motes Books) 10 (Carlow University) and Petals in the Pan (Kind of a Hurricane Press), online at The Written Wardrobe (@ModCloth), The Oklahoma Review, The Journal of Microliterature, the Blue Lake Review, and Gravel Magazine among others, and in such print journals as The Ocean State Review and SLAB.

Betsey Cullen lives in West Chester, PA. Her work has been selected for seversl anthologies published by Kind of a Hurricane Press, and her poem "At Cheever" was one of their 2014 "best poems" selected for Storm Cycle. In addition, poems have appeared in online journals like the Weekly Avocet and in journals like the Broadkill Review. She earned a B.A. from the University of Rochester and an M.A. from Cornell University. Married with two grown children and three granddaughters, she can be reached at ewcullen@yahoo.com.

Graham Curtis is relatively new to creative writing having taken it up in the last year. He is enthusiastic about the possibilities of short and flash fiction. Having worked in the university sector for over thirty years, he now spends considerable time travelling widely.

Oliver Cutshaw has published poetry, short stories, articles, and non-fiction works. He is currently writing a memoir of his father's career as a jockey in the heyday of the horse racing industry. Originally from the East Coast, his works frequently appeared in the literary journals and pop culture weeklies of the Boston area. He now resides in Southern California working as a librarian.

Susan Dale has been published in *WestWard Quarterly, Ken *Again, Penman Review, Inner Art Journal, Garbanzo,* and *Linden Avenue.* In 2007, she won the grand prize for poetry from Oneswan. She has two published chapbooks on the internet: *Spaces Among Spaces* by *languageandculture.org* and *Bending the Spaces of Time* by *Barometric Pressure.*

Tracy Davidson lives in Warwickshire, England, and enjoys writing poetry and flash fiction. Her work has appeared in various publications and anthologies, including: *Mslexia, Poet's Market 2015, Modern Haiku, A Hundred Gourds, Atlas Poetica, The Binnacle, Roundyhouse, Journey to Crone, Ekphrastia Gone Wild* and *In Protest: 150 Poems for Human Rights.*

Lela Marie De La Garza has had work published in *Creepy Gnome, Passion Beyond Words, Black Denim, Yellow Mama, Bewildering Stories,* and *The Western Online.* Her latest novel, *Mistral,* was published in December of 2014. She was born in Denver, CO. in 1943 while her father was serving in WWII. She currently resides in San Antonio, TX. with three and a half cats and a visiting raccoon. *Unfortunately, Lela passed away prior to the publication of this anthology. She will be missed.*

Brindley Hallam Dennis is a writer of short fiction. His stories have been performed by Liars League in London, New York and Hong Kong. He lives on the northern edge of England within sight of three mountain tops and a sliver of Solway Firth. He blogs at www.Bhdandme.wordpress.com/

Julie A. Dickson is a poet and young adult fiction writer living in New Hampshire with three rescued cats. She is the authored of *Bullied into Silence* and other books. Her poems have appeared in various publications including *The Havard Press, The Portsmouth Herald, Poetry Quarterly, Page & Spine, Five Willows Literary Review, The Avocet Nature Poetry Review, Smoky Quartz* and *Van Gogh's Ear*. She is a member of the Poetry Society of New Hampshire, and the Star Island Writers in the Round.

Joseph Dorazio is a prize-winning poet whose poems have been published widely. The author of four volumes of poetry, Dorazio's latest collection, *No Small Effort*, has just been accepted for publication by *Aldrich Press*, and will be available in the fall 2015.

William Doreski lives in Peterborough, New Hampshire, and teaches at Keene State College. His most recent book of poetry is *The Suburbs of Atlantis* (2013). He has published three critical studies, including *Robert Lowell's Shifting Colors*. His essays, poetry, fiction, and reviews have appeared in many journals.

J.K. Durick is a writing teacher at the Community College of Vermont and an online writing tutor. His recent poems have appeared in *Camel Saloon, Black Mirror, Poetry Pacific, Eye on life Magazine,* and *Leaves of Ink.*

Leixyl Kaye Emmerson studied Art History and Poetry in college. She lists motherhood as her biggest accomplishment. Leixyl has published poetry in *Harbinger Asylum* Literary Magazine on several occasions. Her poetry has also been published by Writing Knights Press in their *MIA Warrior Series* and their *365 Anthology Series*. Most recently Leixyl has also contributed to Crisis Chronicles Press *2015 Hessler Street Fair Poetry Anthology*. She is currently working on a book about her family's experience with her son's near fatal car accident. Leixyl is best known for her big heart; she is obsessed with rescuing animals and people alike.

Zach Fechter lives and writes in Wilton, Connecticut. He has been published in Poetry Quarterly Magazine and Kind of a Hurricane Press. He is a graduate of Roanoke College in Salem, Virginia.

Sharon Fedor has spent her professional career as teacher and mentor in Special Education, engaging students who are fascinating and unique while promoting the joy of discovery. She writes poetry and fiction. Her work has been published in *Napalm and Novocain, Halfway down the Stairs, Spellbound, The Camel Saloon*, and *The Moon Magazine* (online), in *Point Mass*, *Legends*, *Conversation with a Christmas Bulb,* the 2013 Best Of Anthology, *Storm Cycle,* and *Petals in the Pan.* She is the second place winner of the 2014 Zero Bone Poetry Prize (Port Yonder Press).

Michael Freveletti is a writer in Chicago. You can read his first published work in an upcoming issue of Allegro Poetry Magazine and Snapdragon Journal this summer. Follow him @mike21an on Twitter for wisdom or because you'd like to increase your Twitter stats.

Jason Gallagher is a contributing editor at Evergreen Review and has been published in both academic publications and the literary journal, *The Otter*. He is also a member of The Unbearables poetry collective. He currently lives in Brooklyn with his wife.

Susan Gardner is an internationally known Santa Fe poet, photographer and painter and the founding editor of Red Mountain Press. Her books of poetry include *Lifted to the Wind, To Inhabit the Felt World,* the bilingual poetry, *Box of Light / Caja de luz,* and *Stone Music: Art and Poetry of Susan Gardner, Intimate Landscapes,* and a memoir, *Drawing the Line.* She has lived and worked in Asia, Mexico and Europe as well as the United States and Canada, with numerous exhibitions in museums and galleries and extensive lectures and readings. She delivered the Cam Memorial Lecture at the New York Public Library, where she was also honored to be granted a year in the Allen Room. She has presented programs at the Freer Gallery of the Smithsonian Institution, the Library of Congress, and the Folger Library, among many others. www.susangardner.org

Brigitte Goetze is a biologist, goat farmer, writer, and lives near Oregon's Coast Range. Her most recent poems can be found in *Agave Literary Journal* and *Mused.* Her web address is: brigittegoetzewriter.weebly.com.

Elissa Gordon mines a childhood spent between New York and New England. She has appeared in print in *Lips, Kind of a Hurricane Press, The Great Falls, An Anthology of Poems about Paterson, New Jersey, Bohemia Art* and *Literary Magazine, NY Underscore, Windmills* (Australia), and online in *Short, Fast & Deadly.*

Ray Greenblatt has been published in: *Pennsylvania Seasons, The Anthology of Magazine Verse & Yearbook of American Poetry,* and *In the West of Ireland.* His book, *Sunspots,* was published by Incline Press (Manchester, England).

John Grey is an Australian poet, US resident. Recently published in New Plains Review, Mudfish and Spindrift with work upcoming in South Carolina Review, Gargoyle, Sanskrit and Louisiana Literature.

Pat Hanahoe-Dosch published her book, Fleeing Back, (a collection of poems by FutureCycle Press) in the summer of 2012. Her poem, "A 21st Century Hurricane: An Assay" was recently nominated for the 2014 Pushcart Prize in Poetry. Her educational background includes an MFA from the University of Arizona in Tucson, Arizona, and she is currently an Associate Professor of English at Harrisburg Area Community College, Lancaster campus. Her poems have been published in previous issues of The Paterson Literary Review, as well as The Atticus Review, War, Art and Literature, Confrontation, The Red River Review, San Pedro River Review, Marco Polo Arts Magazine, Red Ochre Lit, Nervous Breakdown, Quantum Poetry

Magazine, Abalone Moon, Apt, Switched-on Gutenberg, and Paterson: The Poets' City (an anthology edited by Maria Mazziotti Gillan), among others.

William Ogden Haynes is a poet and author of short fiction from Alabama who was born in Michigan and grew up a military brat. He has published three collections of poetry (*Points of Interest;* Uncommon *Pursuits* and Carvings) and one book of short stories (Youthful Indiscretions) all available on Amazon.com. Over a hundred and twenty of his poems and short stories have appeared in literary journals and his work is frequently anthologized.

Eileen Holmes is a member of a Derby poets' group, a reader and a writer who feels that the elements of poetry translate well into the field of short fiction. She has been writing in both genres and her work has been published in the local press and displayed in the Derby Art Gallery.

Ruth Holzer has appeared in previous Kind of a Hurricane anthologies, as well as in a variety of journals including California Quarterly, THEMA, Southern Poetry Review and RHINO. She has published three chapbooks, most recently "A Woman Passing" (Green Fuse Press).

Carol Hornak lives in suburban New Jersey with her husband and has three children. A former preschool teacher, she currently writes poetry, short stories and is working on a novel. She has had stories published in Liquid Imagination, Black Fox Literary Magazine and on the website of Abandoned Towers; poems in *The Battered Suitcase, The Ranfurly Review* and *Bete Noire.*

Susan Martell Huebner lives and writes in Mukwonago, Wisconsin. She loves and appreciates her critique groups and believes a writing community is essential to hone and encourage a writer of any genre.

Liz Hufford is a poet, essayist, and fiction writer residing in Phoenix, Arizona. Her poem "Living with Scorpions" will appear in the inaugural issue of 300 DAYS OF SUN. She is currently working on a young adult novel.

S.E. Ingraham writes from Edmonton, Canada. Successes include publication in Free Fall Lit Mag; The Light Ekphrastic; 2nd nod @ Red Fez; Tom Howard/Margaret Reid poetry contest win; multiple poems in Kind of a Hurricane Press's anthologies; poems in the Poetic Pinup Revue, amongst others. Highlights include Christmas in Paris, a month in Florida including the Palm Beach Poetry Festival and a workshop with the exceptional Thomas Lux. Studying the craft has become a priority. More of her work is available here: http://www.thesoundofthewordnight.blogger.ca/

M.J. Iuppa lives on Red Rooster Farm near the shores of Lake Ontario. Most recent poems, lyric essays and fictions have appeared in the following journals: *Poppy Road Review Black Poppy Review, Digging to the Roots, 2015 Calendar, Ealain, Poetry Pacific Review, Grey Sparrow Press: Snow Jewel Anthology, 100 Word Story, Avocet, Eunoia Review, Festival Writer, Silver Birch Press: Where I Live Anthology,Turtle Island Quarterly, Wild Quarterly, Boyne Berries Magazine (Ireland), The Lake, (U.K.), Punchnel's; forthcoming in Camroc Review, Tar River Poetry, Corvus Review, Clementine Poetry, Postcard* Poetry & *Prose,* among others. She is the Director of the Visual and Performing Arts Minor Program at St. John Fisher College. You can follow her musings on art, writing and sustainability on mjiuppa.blogspot.com.

Evie Ivy is a poet/dancer in the NYC poetry circuit. She hosts one of the longest running poetry series in NYC, the Green Pavilion Poetry Event. She has 3 chapbooks out, including "Selected Cinquains" (Grey Book Press). Her lastest book is "Living in 12-Tone . . . and other poetic forms." Her work has also appeared in various anthologies and websites, including *Levure littéraire, First Literary Review-East, Versewrights* and others.

Diane Jackman has appeared in The Rialto, Outposts, Words-Myth and Story (Happenstance Press) and many other anthologies and magazines. Winner of Liverpool Poetry Festival 2006, Deddington Festival 2014 and Norfolk Prize in Café Writers' competition 2014.

Other works include the libretto for "Pinocchio" for the Kings' Singers/LSO, seven children's books, translated into several languages, children's stories and choral lyrics. She has just completed "Old Land" a series of narratives exploring the lightly-buried past of the countryside, and is now walking the lanes, gathering material for her next sequence.

Juli Jana is a London based poet and artist who uses text to present abstracted, aerial or linear scapes. Slippage and discontinuity are often used as formal strategy in her poetry. She completed a MA Res at Roehampton university and has had work published in various journals. Her two chapbooks, *everybody needs a lunatic* and *ra-t,* are published by Indigo Dreams and Shearsman respectively.

Michael Lee Johnson lived ten years in Canada during the Vietnam era: now known as the Illinois poet, from Itasca, IL. Today he is a poet, freelance writer, photographer who experiments with poetography (blending poetry with photography), and small business owner in Itasca, Illinois, who has been published in more than 875 small press magazines in 27 countries, he edits 10 poetry sites. Michael is the author of The Lost American: "From Exile to Freedom", several chapbooks of poetry, including "From Which Place the Morning Rises" and "Challenge of Night and Day", and "Chicago Poems". He also has over 76 poetry videos on YouTube.

Claire Keyes is the author of *The Question of Rapture* and the chapbook, *Rising and Falling*. Her new book, *What Diamonds Can Do*, was published in 2015. Her poems and reviews have appeared most recently in *Literary Bohemian, Sugar Mule, Crab Orchard Review* and *Blackbird*. She is Professor emerita at Salem State University.

Lori Kiefer teaches creative writing to adults in a mental health day centre and provides counseling support to students at a London University. She is working towards a first collection and also enjoys writing haiku poetry. Her poems are published in several anthologies and she has written several pantomimes.

Phyllis Klein lives and works in the San Francisco Bay area as a therapist and poetry therapist. Her poems have appeared in the *Pharos of Alpha Omega Msedical Society Journal, Emerge* Literary journal, *Qarrtsiluni* online literary magazine, *Silver Birch Press,* on her website, http://www.phyllisklein.com, and in cards and letters. She is very interested in the conversation between poets and readers of poetry. She sees artistic dialogue as an intimate relationship-building process that fosters healing on many levels.

Steve Klepetar has appeared in nine countries, in such journals as *Boston Literary Magazine, Deep Water, Antiphon, Red River Review, Snakeskin, Ygdrasil,* and many others. Several of his poems have been nominated for the Pushcart Prize and Best of the Net. Recent collections include *Speaking to the Field Mice* (Sweatshoppe Publications, 2013), *My Son Writes a Report on the Warsaw Ghetto* (Flutter Press, 2013) and *Return of the Bride of Frankenstein* (Kind of a Hurricane Press).

Julie Kovacs lives in Sarasota, Florida. Her poetry has been published in Rope & Wire, Circle Magazine, Children Churches and Daddies, Because We Write, Illogical Muse, Poems Niederngasse, Aquapolis, The Blotter, Danse Macabre, Silver Blade, The Camel Saloon, Falling Star, Blue and Yellow Dog, Veil, Moria, Nether, and Cherry Bleeds. She is the author of two poetry books: Silver Moonbeams, and The Emerald Grail. Her website is at http://thebiographicalpoet.blogspot.com/

Tricia Knoll is an Oregon poet whose work has appeared in numerous journals and anthologies. Her chapbook Urban Wild is out from Finishing Line Press. She has degrees in literature from Stanford University (BA) and Yale University (MAT). Ocean's Laughter, poems about the northern Oregon coast, comes out from Aldrich Press in late 2015. Website: triciaknoll.com

Kevin Kreiger is an LA-based poet, playwright, and academic/career counselor. His first collection, KAIROS, is due out from Tebot Bach Press in 2015. You can find more of his work at www.inspiritwriting.com.

Veronica Lake is a teacher of Literature and has been for a very long time. She lives in Fremantle, W.A. In 2010 she was awarded a Churchill Fellow for the study of Shakespeare. Her poems have been published in *Cordite, Regime, Cuttlefish* and *Poetry D'Amour*.

Martha Landman writes in North Queensland, Australia. Her work has appeared in various anthologies and in on-line journals including *The New Verse News, Camel Saloon, Eunoia Review, Mused, Jellyfish Whispers, egg* and others.

Mark Lewis has previously had work published in The British Fantasy Society Journal, Life is a Rollercoaster and A Touch of Saccharine anthologies by Kind of a Hurricane Press, Full Fathom Forty, Escape Velocity, Scheherazade, Estronomicon, The Nail, and others. He has also written and performed in pantomimes. He is still working on two novels. Mark is a member of the Clockhouse London Writers. More of Mark's writing can be found at http://syntheticscribe.wordpress.com/

Lyn Lifshin has published over 130 books and chapbooks including 3 from Black Sparrow Press: *Cold Comfort, Before It's Light* and *Another Woman Who Looks Like Me.* Before *Secretariat: The Red Freak, The Miracle,* Lifshin published her prize winning book about the short lived beautiful race horse Ruffian, *The Licorice Daughter: My Year With Ruffian* and *Barbaro: Beyond Brokenness.* Recent books include *Ballroom, All the Poets Who Have Touched Me, Living and Dead. All True, Especially The Lies, Light At the End: The Jesus Poems, Katrina, Mirrors, Persphone, Lost In The Fog, Knife Edge & Absinthe: The Tango Poems.* NYQ books published *A Girl Goes into The Woods.* Also just out: *For the Roses* poems after Joni Mitchell and *Hitchcock Hotel* from Danse Macabre. *Secretariat: The Red Freak, The Miracle.* And

Tangled as the Alphabet,-- The Istanbul Poems from NightBallet Press Just released as well *Malala,* the dvd of *Lyn Lifshin: Not Made of Glass. The Marilyn Poems* was just released from Rubber Boots Press. An update to her Gale Research Autobiography is out: *Lips, Blues, Blue Lace: On The Outside.* Also just out is a dvd of the documentary film about her: *Lyn Lifshin: Not Made Of Glass.* Just out: *Femme Eterna* and *Moving Through Stained Glass: the Maple Poems.* Forthcoming: *Degas Little Dancer* and *The Silk Road.* Her web: www.lynlifshin.com

Lennart Lundh is a poet, short-fictionist, historian, and photographer. His work has appeared internationally since 1965. Len and his wife, Lin, reside in northeastern Illinois.

Hillary Lyon is founder of and editor for the small poetry publishing house, Subsynchronous Press. Her work has appeared in *EOAGH, Shadow Train, Eternal Haunted Summer, Red River Review, Red Fez,* and *Shot Glass Journal,* among others. She lives in southern Arizona.

Don Mager has published several chapbooks and volumes of poetry: *To Track the Wounded One, Glosses, That Which is Owed to Death, Borderings, Good Turns* and *The Elegance of the Ungraspable, Birth Daybook Drive Time* and Russian Riffs. He is retired with degrees from Drake University (BA), Syracuse University (MA) and Wayne State University (PhD). He was the Mott University Professor of English at Johnson C. Smith University from 1998-2004 where he served as Dean of the College of Arts and Letters (2005-2011). As well as a number of scholarly articles, he has published over 200 poems and translations from German, Czech and Russian. He lives in Charlotte, NC. *Us Four Plus Four* is an anthology of translations from eight major Soviet-era Russian poets. It is unique because it tracks almost a half century of their careers by simply placing the poems each wrote to the others in chronological order. The 85 poems represent one of the most fascinating conversations in poems produced by any group of poets in any language or time period. From poems and infatuation and admiration to anger and grief and finally to deep tribute, this anthology invites readers into the unfolding lives of such inimitable creative forces as Anna Akhmatova, Boris Pasternak, Marina Tsvetaeva and Osip Mandelstam.

Stacy Lynn Mar is an American poet. She has authored six collections of poetry, the most recently published is a chapbook of poetry titled Mannequin Rivalry. Stacy is the founder and masthead of the independent women's publisher Pink.Girl.Ink. Press. Hundreds of her poems have been published widely in online/print small press magazine and zines. She is a connoisseur of words and enjoys a life rich in Buddhist values. In her free time she is a practicing Yogi and has been known to devour a whole pot of mocha coffee whilst reading a complete book in one sitting. Stacy also invites you to peruse her personal blog at http://warningthestars.blogspot.com/

Adam Marks is 35 years old. He is married, a father of one. He lives and works in London. He writes speculative fiction. As well as short stories he is also working on a novel. His current influences are William Burroughs, China Mieville, Ward Moore and the SCP Foundation.

Jackie Davis Martin has been included in several current anthologies: *Modern Shorts* (ed. Michelle Richmond*), Love on the Road* (ed. Sam Tranum), *Life is A Rollercoaster*(ed. A.J. Huffman) and *Out Past Loves (*Spruce Mountain*)*. A story recently placed first in *New Millennium Writings* contest and another story second place in *On the Premises*. Her memoir, *Surviving Susan*, was published in 2012. She teaches at City College of San Francisco.

Amanda M. May attained her Master's Degree in Language and Literature from Central Michigan University in 2012. After teaching English for two years in Japan, she returned to America for the next adventure and relocated to Florida in 2015 for work. Her flash fiction appeared in former Kind of a Hurricane Press anthologies, and her poetry, short stories, and essays have been published by various literary magazines. She is currently editing her first novel, her seventh National Novel Writing Month victory, with more seriousness than her former manuscripts.

Bob McNeil recalls reading *A Child's Garden of Verses* at the age of six. As a result, a love of all things poetical bloomed. Later in life, the Imagists and Beats nurtured him. Tenaciously, Bob McNeil tries to compose poetic stun guns and Tasers, weapons for the downtrodden in their effort to trounce oppression. His verses want to be fortresses against despotic politics. After years of being a professional illustrator, spoken word artist and writer, Bob still wants his work to express one cause—justice.

Joan McNerney has been included in numerous literary magazines such as *Camel Saloon, Seven Circle Press, Dinner with the Muse, Blueline, Missing of the Birds,* and included in Bright Hills Press, Kind of A Hurricane Press and Poppy Road Review anthologies. She has been nominated three times for Best of the Net.

Karla Linn Merrifield is a nine-time Pushcart-Prize nominee, and has had over 500 poems appear in dozens of journals and anthologies. She has eleven books to her credit, the newest of which is *Bunchberries, More Poems of Canada* (FootHills Publishing), a sequel to. *Godwit: Poems of Canada* (FootHills Publishing), which received the Eiseman Award for Poetry. She is assistant editor and poetry book reviewer for *The Centrifugal Eye* (www.centrifugaleye.com,), a member of the board of directors of Just Poets (Rochester, NY), and a member of the New Mexico State Poetry Society, the Florida State Poetry Society and TallGrass Writers Guild. Visit her blog, *Vagabond Poet*, at http://karlalinn.blogspot.com.

Dilip Mohapatra is a decorated Navy Veteran started writing poems since the seventies . His poems have appeared in many literary journals of repute in India and abroad. Some of his poems have been featured in the World Poetry Yearbook, 2013 along with the works of 211 contemporary poets from 93 countries and few are lined up for its 2014 Edition due in June 2015. He has two poetry collections titled 'A Pinch of Sun & other poems' and 'Different Shades' to his credit, published by Authorspress India. He holds two masters degrees, in Physics and in Management Studies. He lives with his wife in Pune.

Ralph Monday is Associate Professor of English at Roane State Community College in Harriman, TN., and has published hundreds of poems in over 50 journals. A chapbook, *All American Girl and Other Poems*, was published in July 2014. A book *Empty Houses and American Renditions* was published May 2015 by Aldrich Press. A Kindle chapbook *Narcissus the Sorcerer* was published June 2015 by Odin Hill Press. Website: http://www.ralphmonday.com/

Wilda Morris loves all four seasons, and has poems in numerous journals, anthologies and websites. She is Workshop Chair for Poets & Patrons of Chicago and a former president of the Illinois State Poetry Society. She does workshops in poetry at the Green Lake Conference Center, public libraries and at a Vet's Hospital. Her blog, http://wildamorris.blogspot.com/, provides a monthly contest for other poets.

Carol Murphy is a writer, consultant and speech-language pathologist who has written essays, interviews, stories and poems about children, language development, learning disabilities, the therapeutic and almost mystical influence of animals, and the many ways language, or a lack of it, colors life's experiences. Two of her stories were "Likely Story", published by www.specialeducationadvisor.com , and "Auricle" published in Good Dogs Doing Good. She has also published professional articles and a newsletter for over twenty years and recently won first place for "Tiny Valentine", a poem and subsequent article, "Becoming a Grandmother", published for Times Publishing, an area magazine. She finds daily inspiration for writing through her experiences with the interplay of communication and the many ways lives can go awry, or be set straight, simply by a precise word at a pivotal moment. She lives with her husband, two cats and a horse in Santa Cruz, CA. Writing has been a lifelong passion. A favorite quote is "The word is a microcosm of human consciousness." (Lev Vygotsky)

Joseph Murphy is a professional editor and writer who lives in Michigan. He has had poetry published in a number of journals, including *The Gray Sparrow, Pure Francis* and *The Sugar*

House Review. Murphy is also been a poetry editor for an online literary publication,*Halfway Down the Stairs,* for the past five years.

Lee Nash lives in France and freelances as an editorial designer for a UK publisher. Her poems have appeared or are forthcoming in print and online journals in the UK, the US and France including *The French Literary Review, The Dawntreader, The Lake, Inksweatandtears, Orbis, Sentinel Literary Quarterly,* The World Haiku Review, *Black Poppy Review* and Silver Birch Press. You can find a selection of Lee's poems on her website leenashpoetry.com.

Jude Neale is a Canadian poet, vocalist, spoken word performer and mentor. She publishes frequently in journals, anthologies, and e-zines. She was shortlisted for the Gregory O'Donoghue International Poetry Prize (Ireland), The International Poetic Republic Poetry Prize (U.K),The Mary Chalmers Smith Poetry Prize shortlist (UK), The Wenlock International Poetry Prize (UK), The RCLAS International short story and Poetry Competition (Canada) where she placed second in both categories. She was long listed for the Canadian ReLit Award and the Pat Lowther Award for female writers for her book Only the Fallen Can See (Canada), shortlisted for Editor's Choice, Hurricane Press (USA), highly commended for Sentinel International Poetry Prize (UK) she placed second in the prestigious 2014 Pandora's Literary Collective Poetry Competition and was highly commended in the Carers International (UK). She achieved honorable mention in the Royal City Short Story Competition and was shortlisted twice for The Magpie Poetry Award (Canada). Jude was published in A Kind of Hurricane Presses Best of 2014 Anthology (US). Her latest book, A Quiet Coming of Light, A Poetic Memoir (leaf press), is shortlisted for the 2015 Pat Lowther Memorial Award (best poetry collection by a Canadian woman) and two of its poems were nominated for the coveted Pushcart Prize (US) by two different publishers. One of Jude's poems from her forthcoming manuscript, Midsummer Bewilders the Dog Star, was chosen by the 2015 Guernsey Literary Prize by Britain's Poet Laureate (UK) and will ride with thirty three other winners around the Channel Islands on public transit for a year. The Magpie International Poetry Competition has just informed her that one of her three shortlisted poems has been chosen as a finalist by Vancouver's first Poet Laureate, George McWhirter.

Mary Newell is a writer and educator and lives in the lower Hudson Valley. She has taught literature and writing at the college level. She received a doctorate from Fordham University in American Literature and the Environment, as well as MAs from Teachers College and Columbia University. Her publications include poems published or forthcoming in About Place, First Literary Review East, Jivin' Ladybug, and Howling Dog Press, as well as essays and reviews. Her poem, "The Traffic in Old Ladies" will appear as an honorable mention in the Best of 2014 Anthology of Kind of a Hurricane Press.

Reeve Nicholls is a 16-year-old living in Belper, Derbyshire. This is his first submission for publication.

BZ Niditch is a poet, playwright, and fiction writer. His work is widely published in journals and magazines throughout the world, including: *Columbia: A Magazine of Poetry and Art*; *The Literary Review*; *Denver Quarterly*; *Hawaii Review*; *Le Guepard* (France); *Kadmos* (France); *Prism International*; *Jejune* (Czech Republic); *Leopold Bloom* (Hungary); *Antioch Review*; and *Prairie Schooner*, among others. His latest poetry collections are "Lorca at Seville" and "Captive Cities." He lives in Brookline, Massachusetts.

Suzanne O'Connell lives in Los Angeles where she is a poet and a clinical social worker. Her work can be found in *Forge, Atlanta Review, Crack The Spine, Lummox Journal, Blue Lake Review, G.W. Review, Reed Magazine, Permafrost, Mas Tequila Review, The Round, The Griffin, Sanskrit, Foliate Oak, Talking River, Organs of Vision and Speech Literary Magazine, Willow Review, The Tower Journal, Poetry Super Highway, Thin Air Magazine, Fre&d, The Manhattanville Review, poeticdiversity, The Evansville Review, Serving House Journal, Silver Birch Press, Schuylkill Valley Journal,* and *Licking River Review.* She was a recipient of Willow Review's annual award for 2014 for the poem "Purple Summers." She is a member of Jack Grapes' L.A. Poets and Writers Collective. suzanneoconnell-poet.com

Norman J. Olson is an internationally published poet and artist.

Carl Palmer of Old Mill Road in Ridgeway VA now lives in University Place WA. He has a 2015 contest winning poem riding buses somewhere in Seattle. Carl is a Pushcart Prize and Micro Award nominee.   MOTTO: Long   Weekends   Forever www.authorsden.com/carlpalmer

Joyce Parkes has been published in *The Best Australian Poems (UQP)2005, Overland, Westerly, Meanjin, The Journal of the Australian Irish Heritage Association, the New England Review, Axon,* and in similarly dedicated literary magazines, in print and online, in Australia, the UK, Finland, Canada, Germany, the US, New Zealand and Northern Ireland.

Simon Perchik is an attorney whose poems have appeared in *Partisan Review, The Nation, Osiris, Poetry, The New Yorker*, and elsewhere. His most recent collection is *Almost Rain,* published by River Otter Press (2013). For more information, free e-books and his essay titled "Magic, Illusion and Other Realities" please visit his website at www.simonperchik.com.

Richard King Perkins II is a state-sponsored advocate for residents in long-term care facilities. He lives in Crystal Lake, IL with his wife, Vickie and daughter, Sage. He is a three-time Pushcart nominee and a Best of the Net nominee. Writing for six years, his work has appeared in more than a thousand publications including The Louisiana Review, Bluestem, Emrys Journal, Sierra Nevada Review, Roanoke Review, The Red Cedar Review and The William and Mary Review. He has poems forthcoming in Hawai'i Review, Sugar House Review, Plainsongs, Free State Review and Texas Review.

Georgia Ressmeyer is a New York native who has lived happily in Wisconsin since 1974, first as an attorney with legal services and public defender programs in Milwaukee, now as a poet and promoter of art & poetry collaborations in Sheboygan. Twice a winner of grants from the Wisconsin Arts Board, she has published fiction, numerous poems, and a poetry chapbook, *Today I Threw My Watch Away* (Finishing Line Press), which received an award from the Wisconsin Fellowship of Poets. Her full-length poetry collection, *Waiting to Sail,* was published by Black River Press in 2014.

Pippa Rowen is from Derby in England. She has a professional background in social research; thus far her writing has been academic. She has edited a collection of war stories and poetry entitled 'Sacrifice Remembered: reflections on 100 years of war by the people of Derbyshire.' Her introduction to creative writing was through a course. Her flash fiction story 'England Through the Seasons' is her first piece of creative writing since high school.

Tom Russell has a short list of publication credits and has thus far been unable to attain the title of Poet-In-Residence of his living room. He works at the public library in Omaha, Nebraska.

Mary Salen writes poetry from her farm house in the historic Oley Valley, Pennsylvania, where she lives with her husband and five children. Some of Ms. Salen's poetry has previously appeared in Kind of a Hurricane Press, High Coupe.

Paul Sasges comes from a unique western Canadian experience living most of his life on the Pacific Ocean in Vancouver, B.C. Paul also spent five years at sea as a marine officer in the Canadian Coast Guard, first as a cadet in Sydney Nova Scotia, then as a watch-keeper in St John's Newfoundland. He has two children and is studying Publishing, and World Literature at Simon Fraser University.

Francesca Sasnaitis is a Melbourne-based writer and artist, currently embarked on a PhD in Creative Writing at the University of Western Australia. Her poetry, fiction and reviews have most recently appeared in *Australian Book Review,*

Cordite, Southerly, Sydney Review of Books, The Trouble with Flying and other stories and *Westerly*.

Emily Jo Scalzo has an MFA in Fiction from California State University, Fresno. She currently resides in Muncie, Indiana, and is an assistant professor at Ball State University. Her work has been published in *Mobius: The Journal of Social Change, The Mindful Word, Ms. Fit Magazine*, and *Third Wednesday*.

Zvi A. Sesling is a prize winning poet, and has published in numerous magazines. He edits *Muddy River Poetry Review* and publishes "Muddy River Books." He authored *King of the Jungle* (Ibbetson Street Press, 2010) and a chapbook *Across Stones of Bad Dreams* (Cervena Barva, 2011). His volume, *Fire Tongue,* is due from Cervena Barva Press.

Jo Simons teaches piano and Music Together in Madison, WI. She started writing poetry 5 years ago when she thought her 93-year old father was dying. The poems helped tremendously to deal with the stress of that. He's now 98 and in great health! And I became a poet.

Rosemary Marshall Staples is a NH Poet and songwriter with a humorous side. Her work has appeared in Spotlight magazine, Poet's Touchstone and Piscataqua Poems. She features at local venues with her poetry and music, is a member of The Poetry Society of NH, and The Writers in the Round at Star Island.

Tom Sterner wrestles with creativity: graphic art, music, photography, & WORD. A native Coloradoan, he lives in Denver. Tom's artwork, music, photography, & written word have been published in magazines & on the internet by various folk, including *Howling Dog Press/Omega, Carpe Articulum Literary Review, Skyline Literary Review, The Storyteller, & Flashquake*. Published work includes five novels: *~momma's rain~, ~spiders 'n snakes~, ~gordian objective~, ~after earth~, ~cranial loop~* & the epic book-length poem *~quodlibet~*. He is winner of the Marija Cerjak Award for Avant-Garde/Experimental Writing & was nominated for the Pushcart Prize in

2006 & 2008. email: wordwulf@gmail.com website: http://wordwulf.com

Jeanine Stevens poetry has appeared in Pearl, Earth's Daughters, North Dakota Review, Evansville Review, Perfume River, Tipton Poetry Review and Arabesque. Her latest chapbook, *Needle in the Sea*, was published by Tiger's Eye Press in 2014. She has awards from the Bay Area Poet's Coalition, Stockton Arts Commission and Ekphrasis. Raised in Indiana, she now divides her time between Sacramento and Lake Tahoe.

Emily Strauss has an M.A. in English, but is self-taught in poetry, which she has written since college Over 250 of her poems appear in a wide variety of online venues and in anthologies, in the U.S. and abroad. The natural world is generally her framework; she also considers the stories of people and places around her and personal histories. She is a semi-retired teacher living in California.

Smita Sriwastav is an M.B.B.S. doctor with a passion for poetry and literature. She has always expressed her innermost thoughts and sentiments through the medium of poetry. A feeling of inner tranquility and bliss captures her soul whenever she pens her verse. Nature has been the most inspiring force in molding the shape of her writings. She has published two books Efforts and Pearls of Poetry and has published poems in journals like the Rusty Nail (Rule of Survival, Conversations) and Contemporary Literary Review India (spring lingers),four and twenty, Paradise Review, Literary Juice, Dark Matter Journal, Torrid Literature, Milk Sugar, vox poetica, the Shine Journal, Daily Love, Rainbow Rose, Life As An [Insert Label Here], Inclement Poetry Magazine, Red Poppy Review, Blast Furnace and many more and one of her poems "Unsaid Goodbyes" was published in an anthology called 'Inspired by Tagore' published by Sampad and British Council.One of her poems was published in the anthology A Golden Time for Poetry and in other anthologies by kind of a hurricane press, viz. Something's Brewing, Storm Cycle 2013, Tic Toc, Just a Touch of Saccharine, Life is a Roller

Coaster and Switch the Difference. She has written poetry all her life and aims to do so forever. Her poetry can be read online on her blog, Rain-Chimes~My Poetry Blog, http://drsmitasriwas280. wordpress.com/

Neelamani Sutar is an Mathematics scholar.He writes since his childhood days. He is a Prasar Bharti Lyricist & Playwright. He has written for a number of National & International Periodicals. Some of his best seller anthologies are Something Happened On The Way To Heaven: Penguin India, Purple Hues & I Am A Woman: Sanmati Publishers & Distributers, The Pink Throne: Ink Lovers India, The Untold Love Stories: Authors' Ink India, Nationalism & Independence: Airavat Publishers' quirelle: Rejected Stuff, Deep Tales: Edited By Lulu & many more in Indian Languages. He lives in Cuttack, Odisha, India. E-mail ID-sutarneelamani@gmail.com .

Fanni Sütő is a writer, poet, dreamer in her mid-twenties, who believes in fairy tales even if they are dark, disenchanted and deconstructed. She writes about everything which comes in her way or goes bump in the night. She has been published in Hungary, the US, the UK and Australia. www.inkmapsandmacarons.com

Anne Swannell lives in Victoria where she paints scenery for local theatres, and smashes plates, tea-pots, cups, and saucers to make mosaics. Anne's poetry has been published in various literary journals and she has three books of poetry: *Drawing Circles on the Water* (self-published, 1989), *Mall* (Rowan Books, Edmonton, 1991) and *Shifting* (Ekstasis Editions, Victoria, 2008).

Marianne Szlyk is a professor at Montgomery College and the editor of The Song Is... Recently, she published her second chapbook, I Dream of Empathy, with Flutter Press. Her first (Listening to Electric Cambodia, Looking Up at Trees of Heaven) was published by Kind of a Hurricane Press. Her poems have appeared in Long Exposure, ken*again, Of/with, bird's thumb, Indus Streams, Taj Mahal Review, Silver Birch Press' Where I Live Series, Jellyfish Whispers, Napalm and Novocaine, Poppy Road Review, and other online and print venues including Kind of a Hurricane Press' anthologies. "The Holly Tree in

Summer" was inspired by Martin Willits, Jr.'s poems on Celtic astrology, which appeared in Jellyfish Whispers. What a small world!

Susan Tally has appeared in several magazines, *Melancholy Hyperbole, Birds Piled Loosely, Clementine and upcoming issues of Loveliest Magazine and Oatmeal.* Susan lives in New York City, where she has participated in a series of poetry workshops. She works with young children in public schools.

Sarah Thursday calls Long Beach, California, her home, where she advocates for local poets and poetry events. She runs a Long Beach-focused poetry website called CadenceCollective.net, co-hosts a monthly reading with G. Murray Thomas, and founded Sadie Girl Press as a way to help publish local and emerging poets. Her first full-length poetry collection, All the Tiny Anchors, is available now. A second poetry CD with music and a new full length book are in the works! Find and follow her to learn more on SarahThursday.com, Facebook, or Twitter.

Dennis Trujillo is a former soldier and middle/high school math teacher who happens to love poetry. Most recent selections are forthcoming or already published with *Atlanta Review, Ascent, Agave, THEMA, Slant, 3Elements Review, Your Daily Poem, Wild Goose Poetry Review, Silver Birch Press,* and *Snapdragon: A Journal of Art and Healing.* He runs and does yoga each morning for grounding, focus, and for the sheer joy of it.

Tesia Tsai is currently a graduate student at Brigham Young University, studying creative writing. She hopes to one day write novels for children and young adults. In her free time, Tesia enjoys reading, writing, watching animated movies, and daydreaming about her next trip to Disneyland.

Marion Turner lives in London and writes prose and poetry on a regular basis. She has had poems published in the Pre-Raphaelite Society's Review and in the e-book, Dictionary of Made-Up Words, published by English Pen. Published prose includes a short story in Wordland 3 and flash fiction in Graffiti issue 15. Further flash fiction won the prize in the competition, London Journey. She is also writes lyrics with a local composer.

Loretta Diane Walker is a multiple Pushcart nominee. She has published two collections of poetry and her manuscript In This House is forth coming in 2015. Loretta was recently named "Statesman in the Arts" by the Heritage Council of Odessa. Walker's work has appeared in numerous publications, most recently *Her Texas, Texas Poetry Calendar 2015, Pushing Out the Boat International Journal, San Pedro River Review, Illya's Honey, Red River Review, Diversity: Austin International Poetry Festival, Boundless Poetry: Rio Grande Valley International Poetry Festival, Pushing the Envelope: Epistolary Poems, Perception Literary Magazine, and is forthcoming in Connecticut River Review, The Texas Poetry Calendar 2016, and Siblings: Our First Macrocosm.* Her manuscript Word Ghetto won the 2011 Bluelight Press Book Award. She teaches music in Odessa, Texas. Loretta received a BME from Texas Tech University and earned a MA from The University of Texas of the Permian Basin.

Toren Wallace currently teaches at the Literary Arts Center, Beyond Baroque, in Venice, California. He is a candidate in the MFA Creative Writing: Poetry program at California State University, Long Beach. His work has appeared in The Portland Review, American Mustard, Lip Stick Party Mag, and Poetic Diversity: Los Angeles.

Mercedes Webb-Pullman graduated from IIML Victoria University Wellington with MA in Creative Writing in 2011. Her poems and the odd short story have appeared online, in print and in her books *Food 4 Thought, Numeralla Dreaming, After the Danse, Ono, Looking for Kerouac, Tasseography, Bravo Charlie Foxtrot* and *Collected poems 2008 - 2014.* She lives on the Kapiti Coast, New Zealand. www.benchpress.co.nz

Mary L. Westcott has been writing poetry for more than 25 years. She received an MA in Writing from Johns Hopkins University in 2010. She has been published in more than 55 literary journals. She has published 6 books of poetry, including the latest from Balboa Press, called *Fluttering on Earth*, a poetic memoir. She retired from the National Institutes of Health, and lives in Central Florida.

Joanna M. Weston is married, has two cats, multiple spiders, a herd of deer, and two derelict hen-houses. Her middle-reader, *Those Blue Shoes*, was published by Clarity House Press, and her poetry, *A Summer Father*, was published by Frontenac House of Calgary. Her eBooks found at her blog: http://www.1960willowtree.wordpress.com/

Dan Wilcox is the host of the Third Thursday Poetry Night at the Social Justice Center in Albany, N.Y. and is a member of the poetry performance group "3 Guys from Albany". As a photographer, he claims to have the world's largest collection of photos of unknown poets. You can read his Blog about the Albany poetry scene at dwlcx.blogspot.com.

Martin Willitts, Jr. has been in many Kind Of Hurricane anthologies and they have two of his poetry web books. He won the one time 2014 International Dylan Thomas Award. He has 28 chapbooks and 8 full-length collections of poetry. Forthcoming collections include "*Martin Willitts Jr, Greatest Hits*" (Kattywompus Press), "*How to Be Silent*" (FutureCycle Press), "*God Is Not Amused With What You Are Doing In Her Name*" (Aldrich Press), and "*Hearing the Inaudible*" (Poetica Publishing).

Laura Madeline Wiseman is the author of twenty books and chapbooks and the editor of *Women Write Resistance: Poets Resist Gender Violence* (Hyacinth Girl Press). Her recent books are *Drink* (BlazeVOX Books), *Wake* (Aldrich Press), *Some Fatal Effects of Curiosity and Disobedience* (Lavender Ink), *The Bottle Opener* (Red Dashboard), and the collaborative book *The Hunger of the Cheeky Sisters* (Les Femmes Folles) with artist Lauren Rinaldi. Her work has appeared in *Prairie Schooner, Margie, Mid-American Review, Ploughshares,* and *Calyx*.

Phil Wood works in a statistics office. He enjoys working with numbers and words. Published work can be found in various publications including: *Sein und Werden, The Centrifugal Eye, London Grip, The Lampeter Review*, the anthology *Wherever You Roam* (pub.Pankhearst).

Mantz Yorke lives in Manchester, England. His poems have appeared in *Butcher's Dog, Dactyl, Dawntreader, Lunar Poetry, Popshot, Prole, Revival* and *The Brain of Forgetting* magazines, in e-magazines and in anthologies in the UK, Ireland and the US.

Changming Yuan is an 8-time Pushcart nominee, grew up in rural China, started to learn English at 19 and published several monographs on translation before moving to Canada. Currently co-editing *Poetry Pacific* with Allen Qing Yuan in Vancouver, Yuan has poetry appearing in 1009 literary publications across 31 countries, including *Best Canadian Poetry, BestNewPoemsOnline,* and *Threepenny Review.*

About The Editors

A.J. Huffman has published eleven solo chapbooks and one joint chapbook through various small presses. Her new poetry collections, *Another Blood Jet* (Eldritch Press), *A Few Bullets Short of Home* (mgv2>publishing), *Butchery of the Innocent* (Scars Publications) and *Degeneration* (Pink Girl Ink) are now available from their respective publishers and amazon.com. She has an additional poetry collection forthcoming: *A Bizarre Burning of Bees* (Transcendent Zero Press). She is a three-time Pushcart Prize nominee, a two-time Best of Net nominee, and has published over 2300 poems in various national and international journals, including *Lableter, The James Dickey Review, Bone Orchard, EgoPHobia,* and *Kritya.* She is also the founding editor of Kind of a Hurricane Press. www.kindofahurricanepress.com.

April Salzano teaches college writing in Pennsylvania and is currently working on a memoir on raising a child with autism along with several collections of poetry. Her work has been twice nominated for a Pushcart Award and has appeared in journals such as *The Camel Saloon, Centrifugal Eye, Deadsnakes, Visceral Uterus, Salome, Poetry Quarterly, Writing Tomorrow* and *Rattle.* Her chapbook, *The Girl of My Dreams,* is available from Dancing Girl Press (https://dulcetshop.myshopify.com/collections/frontpage/product s/the-girl-of-my-dreams-april-salzano). More of her work can be read at http://aprilsalzano.blogspot.com/

Made in the USA
Lexington, KY
30 October 2015